Feed My Shepherds

Feed My Shepherds

Spiritual Healing and Renewal
for Those in Christian Leadership

Flora Slosson Wuellner

UPPER
ROOM BOOKS
NASHVILLE

FEED MY SHEPHERDS
Spiritual Healing and Renewal for Those in Christian Leadership
© 1998 by Flora Slosson Wuellner
All rights reserved.

The Upper Room Web Site: http://www.upperroom.org

Cover design: Michele Wetherbee
Cover transparency: © Byron Jorjorian
First printing: January 1998

Library of Congress Cataloging-in-Publication
Wuellner, Flora Slosson.
    Feed my shepherds: spiritual healing and renewal for those in Christian leadership / Flora Slosson Wuellner.
            p.   cm.
    Includes bibliographical references.
    ISBN 0-8358-0845-9
    1. Clergy—Religious life. 2. Jesus Christ—Appearances. 3. Spiritual life—Christianity. I. Title.
    BV4011.6.W84   1998   97-26888
    248.8 ' 92—dc21   CIP

Printed in the United States of America on acid-free paper

This book is lovingly dedicated to

my husband, Wilhelm,

who has nourished and enriched my life, as we
have "shepherded" one another.

Contents

INTRODUCTION 10

1   Spiritual Desolation in Christian Leadership 16
     ...weeping outside the tomb (John 20:11).

2   The Heart of Christian Spirituality. 30
     Jesus said to her, "Mary" (John 20:16).

3   Spiritual Release or Spiritual Abuse?. 44
     *The doors...were locked...Jesus came and stood
     among them (John 20:19).*

4   Incarnational Spirituality. 60
     "Touch me and see" (Luke 24:39).

5   Depth Healing: The Leader's Urgent Need 74
     *He showed them his hands and his side
     (John 20:20).*

6   Walking with Christ to Deep, Wounded Memories . 96
     *Jesus himself came near and went with them
     (Luke 24:15).*

7   Spiritual Exhaustion and Depth Renewal 108
     *Jesus...took the bread and gave it to them
     (John 21:13).*

8   Our Deepest Flaw, Our Greatest Gift 128
     "Simon..., do you love me?" (John 21:15).

9   Spiritual Protection in Toxic Relationships 140
     *"Stay here in the city until you have been clothed
     with power" (Luke 24:49).*

10 Spiritual Discipline or Spiritual Response? 162
"And remember, I am with you always"
(Matthew 28:20).

11 Breath, Bread, and Blessing 172
Lifting up his hands, he blessed them (Luke 24:50).

NOTES 189

Introduction

$\mathcal{T}$HE TITLE OF THIS BOOK came to me with startling clarity as soon as I hung up the phone. I had been talking with my editor about a book written especially for those in active Christian leadership. By the time we finished our first talk, I knew what the title had to be.

I was surprised. Usually I have a terrible time deciding on a book title. Also I realized that to some people "shepherd" might seem an irrelevant metaphor, considering that most of us live in cities and do not work with sheep! I wondered too about the gender implication of *shepherd*. Would that term be a stumbling block to some? Moreover, Jesus never said in so many words, "Feed my shepherds." He told Peter to feed the *sheep*. I uneasily thought of that great pastoral chapter Ezekiel 34, which contains many grim words about shepherds who are overly concerned with feeding themselves! How could I justify this title?

But the title felt deeply authentic, as well as very surprising. Guidance often feels that way. *Shepherd* is biblically rooted and widely used and accepted as a metaphor in the art, song, and preaching of our Christian communities. The word *pastor*, for example, means "a shepherd." Jesus spoke of himself as the "good shepherd." That image still carries significant power for most of us.

I recognize the problem of the gender connotation. But I also remember my years of ministry in the sheep ranching country of Wyoming and Idaho. *Shepherd* was the word used either for a man or a woman who cared for sheep. For many people, *shepherd* remains an acceptable and understood symbol for a care-giving religious leader. But I do invite any reader troubled by its use to substitute another metaphor.

Most of all, I felt the strong conviction, to the point of urgency, that God deeply cares about the well-being and sustenance of the active men and women, the leaders within the Christian communities, who "feed the sheep" in so many diverse ways. The four Gospel Resurrection narratives reveal the intense, healing relationship between the risen Jesus and his disciples, the future shepherds of the new-born Christian church. For me, these Easter stories have become a paradigm of the sustaining bond meant to exist between the living Jesus Christ and all who work in the power of that name.

These workers include not only the professional Christian leaders: pastors, chaplains, counselors, missionaries, church and conference administrators, educators, church-related social workers, and other professional branches. Also included are all active *lay leaders*, the men and women involved in shepherding work of every possible variety among the hungry "sheep" of the church and the world. Christian lay leaders rightly refer to their special calling as ministry.

This book's focus is *not* meant to minimize the deep bond between Jesus the Christ and all the loving, dedicated Christians of the church who are not presently serving in leadership roles. The church is the communal body of all who love Jesus Christ, not just the leaders or those in active roles. At times, every Christian leader needs to move *out* of an active role in order to experience a time of fallowness, rest, and quietude within the great enfolding presence of the church. That time of fallowness and quietude is no less within the radiant empowering communion with the living Christ. God calls all of us to be living branches within the living vine of Christ.

While all Christians need nurture and sustenance, the active Christian leader who encounters spiritual and emotional stress daily has special, urgent needs. If the shepherd is not fed along with the sheep, that inner hunger and fatigue, those unhealed hurts can cause the shepherd to do great, unconscious harm to those within his or her care.

Jesus focused on these special needs of the future shepherds of the church during those forty days after his resurrection. He deepened his tender bond with them. He ministered to their fear, guilt, doubts, fatigue, and hurts. He encountered their wounds in his risen spiritual body that carried his wounds as well as his light. He "fed" the shepherds, *not* as mere instruments but as beloved friends. "Having loved his own who were in the world, he loved them to the end" (John 13:1).

The Easter stories recorded in the four Gospels shine forth the different aspects of the Resurrection relationship. In Matthew we find the burning empowerment and awesome mandate of the Great Commission. In Mark we experience with almost breathless wonder the radical new beginning that shines forth in the Resurrection drama.

The writer of Luke/Acts startlingly fleshes out the Resurrection experience with many tender human touches. Here we encounter the risen Jesus sharing both food and thoughts with his friends. The Gospel writer intensifies the personal bonding with the Christ; we receive the new empowered gift that enables us to fulfill the Great Commission.

The witness and vision of John's Gospel call us to enter more deeply into that mystery of the union between the living Jesus Christ and the believer. We share the *shalom*, that vibrant word of peace and wholeness spoken in the locked room on Resurrection night. Our empty nets are filled from the lake; the fire and food are prepared for us on the beach. Our inner healing moves to a deeper place, and Jesus Christ gives us the mandate: "Feed my sheep."

All these aspects of the Resurrection relationship become the daily bread of every Christian. But if the Christian leader lacks this sustenance, he or she begins to dry up, wither, and die at the very root. Out of this urgency this book has grown.

In the first chapter I share my own story of spiritual dryness and desolation in the early years of my ministry. Throughout the book I often draw not only on my own experiences but also on those of other Christians in leadership.

There are certain things that this book is *not*. It is not a manual of special spiritual methodology, though I share many suggested prayers, reflections, and meditations; and I occasionally refer to excellent books on methodology.

It is not a book that focuses on mystical experiences, though most of us, as we continue to grow and unfold within the divine-human relationship, will eventually have such experiences. Often we do not recognize them for what they are, because they seem so natural and spontaneous.

This book does not reflect on communal or liturgical spirituality, significant and vital though it is. However, I believe the deepening of our own spiritual wholeness and healing will greatly influence our liturgies.

This *is* a book that seeks to explore the foundations of healthy, nonabusive spirituality; a book that reflects on the spiritual and emotional needs, the unhealed wounds and fatigue of the Christian leader within his or her many demanding, draining relationships. Above all, this book reflects on the spiritual developmental unfolding and deepening of the Resurrection relationship with the living Christ.

Some of the material in this book represents new frontiers in my own growth. Other aspects of the material I have developed in my earlier books but have reworked them to address the specific needs of the "shepherds."

I invite you to take and use what you need; feel free to put the rest aside. The *only* authority is that of your own heart bonded with the heart of Jesus Christ. Respect for your freedom, your timing, and the uniqueness of your personal response to God is the very essence of Christian spirituality (though too often violated). Modify the suggested meditations and metaphors according to your own need, your own guidance.

Sometimes I combine reflection questions with the guided

meditation at the conclusion of each chapter. You may prefer to separate these questions from the actual meditation.

Each meditation offers alternate ways of experience: visualization, inner or outer verbal prayer, and bodily response to God. You may feel more drawn to one way than to another, or you may wish to experience them all.

If you are leading a group or an individual in any of these guided meditations, make it clear and explicit that each person is free *not* to participate, is free to withdraw at any time, is free inwardly to stop the process and enter into some other way of praying, is free to change any imagery or metaphor that causes discomfort. When you read a meditation to a group or individual, read very slowly with long pauses for silent reflection. Often use such releasing words as: "This may be all you need right now," and "If you feel ready to continue...." Always respect inner resistances and defenses, both in yourself and others.

As I have felt guided and blessed in this writing, may you also feel blessed in the reading.

1

Spiritual Desolation in Christian Leadership

...weeping outside the tomb
(John 20:11).

*I*N THE MIDDLE OF THE FUNERAL SERVICE I was leading, I suddenly realized I did not believe what I was saying. It had been a tragic and traumatic death: an eighteen-year-old boy—an only child, college bound that fall, enthusiastic member of our little Chicago church—killed in an auto accident while riding to a church camp where he was a summer counselor.

I spoke of the limitless love of God, the closeness of the Comforter, the life eternal within God's heart as I looked at the faces of his parents, our church members, his weeping school friends; but as I spoke, a grim realization grew within me that I didn't really believe what I was saying. God's love, closeness, and power to comfort suddenly seemed so dim and unreal.

Obviously I said nothing of this to the grieving congregation. Nothing would have been more cruel. I went on with the service, and later quite a number of people told me how my words had comforted them. For this I thanked...well...God, I supposed. I drove back to the parsonage knowing that I needed lots of time and space to think through and try to understand what had happened to me.

How had this loss of faith crept up on me without my even suspecting it? I had been drawn into the ministry in my early teens because of the healing and radiant awareness of "the glory of God in the face of Jesus Christ" (2 Cor. 4:6). Prayer was a joy and refreshment in those days. I had been an enthusiastic member, then leader, in our university church youth group, which taught me many skills for later ministry. I had experienced the pastoral field for four summers in the Rocky Mountain area during the years of theological school. I spent four summers in Wyoming and Idaho: two with rural churches, one with a city church, and one organizing and launching a new community church for the Board of Home Missions. All were ecstatic experiences. I entered my full-time pastorate in a small inner-city church in Chicago with overflowing joy and energy. Where had all my enthusiasm, joy, and energy gone? Why was there now this absence and emptiness where there had been such radiant, vital, living presence? I felt, indeed, like Mary, "weeping outside the tomb."

It took me quite a while to understand this shift. I had to be totally honest with myself, which is never easy. Eventually I admitted that most of the joy and savor had gone out of my ministry a long time back. This is not the sort of thing one wants to admit. For some time I had been working even harder to avoid facing the fact that many of my ministerial tasks had become boring and burdensome. Sunday services had become repetitive ceremonies with little vital meaning. I felt restless and drained by meeting the emotional and spiritual needs of my congregation.

I looked at my prayer life: That had stopped almost entirely! I prayed from the pulpit, of course, and was always careful to make my pulpit prayers theologically articulate and correct. I prayed with the sick—they expected it. *It didn't accomplish much,* I thought drearily, *but after all it is part of my job.* But what of my personal prayer life? It had become just one more professional duty among all too many other ministerial duties. I could postpone this duty because no one would know about it but myself and God—and so far, God did not seem to object!

I began to see some connections between my bereft prayer life and my spiritual dryness; I probed deeper. When had I stopped praying? I had certainly prayed with fervent joy as a teenager, at church camps, and later as a student in my summer pastorates. I had even prayed in theological seminary! That had not been easy, because (at the time anyway) a personal prayer life was not a major priority in theological circles.

To be sure, the seminary offered a daily chapel service of a rather formal nature but no courses in personal spirituality. The seminary considered that subject to be an aspect of homiletics and liturgy. The well-known and much-loved theologian Daniel Day Williams, the one professor who concerned himself with the spiritual nurture of students, organized a weekly early-morning communion service and met with us occasionally for spiritual discussion and prayer. The other members of the faculty and administration approved but ignored this effort. But for a handful of us students, it was like an oasis in the desert.

Sometimes a few of us would gather in a dorm room, light a candle stuck in an empty wine bottle, and share an hour of meditation. And some of us began a daily early-morning prayer hour in a huge, empty church nearby. The church was appallingly cold, dark, and cavernous at seven o'clock on winter mornings. That effort lasted exactly one week!

The seminary not only offered no classes on spirituality; it offered no classes on the minister's emotional health. The church required no psychological screening for ministerial candidates forty years ago. The mere fact that you had chosen the ministry and had been an active church member was evidence enough that you had what it took. Our seminary taught, and taught well, how to counsel others, how to listen to others below the verbal level. Students learned how to respond to the unspoken as well as spoken needs, feelings, questions. (The Carl Rogers approach was then coming into its own.) But no one taught us how to listen to ourselves, to our own inner needs and wounds. The great thing was to be "a man for others."

Service to God and to others, an intelligent theology, a working knowledge of scripture, a trained ability to preach and lead meaningful worship services, an ability to organize and lead a church community, a reasonable concern for social justice—these competencies were supposed to be enough to provide us with our ministerial identity. At that time, the late 1950s, the   great emphasis was on church growth, church building, inner-city missions, and outreach to rural areas. The huge popular surge back to the institutional church resulted in ministerial training to meet this challenge of church management. There was little or no emphasis on the spiritual hunger of a congregation.

No ministers' retreats were offered to those of us serving in the parish. At that time, our denomination did not have such priorities. Also at that time, no committees on the ministry or pastoral networks offered comfort and counsel to ministers and their families. We were out there "to cut the mustard." The alternatives were to leave the ministry or to remain (perhaps for life) in a depressed, though hidden, state of low-grade burnout.

When I received the call to my first full-time pastorate, the president of my theological seminary called me into his office. Sitting behind his huge, polished desk, he looked me in the eye and said bluntly, "Flora, decide now if you are going to this church as their shepherd or as their little pet lamb!"

He meant well. Women ministers were still a rarity, and I was rather young to be the sole pastor of even a small church. I responded to his challenge, determined to establish my ministerial authority and imperturbability at once. I would be the church's leader, shepherd, authority, unending fount of love and inspiration. I would attend to every need, every wound, and every committee!

No one asked, nor did I ask, how I was going to be fed, sustained, and renewed. I assumed that my early spiritual experiences would last a lifetime. And surely my weekly preaching and leadership of public worship would feed my spiritual needs. Surely my pastoral counseling would bring me whatever emotional support was necessary.

No one had taught me that if the branch detaches itself from the vine and tries to be a vine itself, it will wither and die. No one had pointed out that if a shepherd is not fed as well as the sheep, that shepherd will begin to starve and may end up *devouring* the sheep. In our hunger, we feed on others in many covert as well as overt ways! Or perhaps a shepherd determined to "die to self" may allow the sheep to devour him or her! That too can happen in many grim ways. We have all seen (and some-times experienced) ministries that have become a hemorrhage, a dying, rather than a fulfilling and fulfilled life.

I had never thought to take personally that powerful, poignant Resurrection story in John's Gospel: The risen Christ builds the fire, cooks, and serves breakfast to the disciples; he heals Peter's guilt and shame—all *before* he sends them out to feed the hungry sheep of the world. (See John 21:4-19.)

Because I had so misunderstood the deep meanings of prayer and personal relationship with Christ, personal prayer was the first thing to go down the drain. Praying had been easy for me before I entered full-time ministry, but I had not learned how to pray when overwhelmed with pastoral tasks that I never delegated. Nor had I realized the unique problem that arises when we identify our spiritual life with our professional work. When we connect spirituality with our daily job and our finan-cial support, spirituality can easily become just another respon-sibility, more of the same old thing. The professional Christian leader is not the only one who often experiences this malaise. Many active laypeople—responsible, overworked church leaders —feel this same strain and depletion to the extent that they drop out of church altogether. Sunday was no breakfast on the beach for them either.

So where could I be fed on the beach? Where could I find that deep rest and nourishment for body and spirit? In prayer? Hardly. Anything but! Or so it seemed to me then and to sev-eral other ministers I knew.

Outwardly things were going well. My little church, one of the smallest in the conference, grew in membership, financial independence, and vitality. The members responded to me, their first full-time pastor in thirty years, with eager love. Looking back, I realize now that undoubtedly some of those members had rich spiritual lives, but I could not share even a small part of my spiritual confusion with them. I could not share with them first because I did not clearly realize what was happening to me; second, I worried too much about becoming their "little pet lamb" even to think of talking about my needs. Then came that funeral service.

> They made me keeper of the vineyards,
> but my own vineyard I have not kept! (Song of Sol. 1:6).

> When its boughs are dry, they are broken (Isa. 27:11).

As I explored the death (or sleep) of my faith, I realized that *any* personal relationship will wither and lose faith if personal, depth communication fails. This happens between spouses, between parents and children, between best friends. The relationship that began in joy and vitality becomes a bore and burden or meaningless routine. This loss of vitality in relationship can also happen between the human being and God. God does not withdraw, but we can—and do. Then the shining joy of ministry withers away.

But I still did not know how one could pray when beset with so many tasks. Would it be just a matter of grim determination? of willpower? Who would help me get started again? In those days, spiritual direction was not an option among mainline Protestants. It was considered to be a monastic practice. I knew of no spiritual retreat centers. We ministers were hesitant to talk frankly among ourselves about the problem of our loss of spiritual vitality. (Too dangerous from the perspective of ecclesiastical politics. We weren't supposed to have such problems!) Those who did talk about it usually had no helpful answers.

Of course, there were books out there that would teach me all about prayer disciplines, I assured myself. I bought some of them and tried a few of the suggested methods. Most of the books assumed the necessity of early morning rising and meditation before breakfast. I was not (and never have been) an early-morning person. Most of the books assumed the necessity of a specially designated hour each day for prayer, going through the unvarying routine of adoration, confession, petition, intercession, and commitment. But I am not and never have been one who does the same thing at the same time every day, year after year. I tried, but it never lasted. Sadly I concluded that I was not suited to prayer disciplines.

Most books on the mystical experience drew heavily upon the spiritual classics of earlier centuries. Many of these books reflected a monastic approach to life and a world-denying, ego-slaying attitude that contradicted everything I had ever learned about healthy and complex human nature. Some wonderful exceptions were the books of Evelyn Underhill, Rufus Jones, Thomas Kelly, and Douglas V. Steere. They served as a light in the tunnel, but by that time the whole spiritual undertaking seemed burdensome and tiring.

I decided to try to experience the essence of prayer through deeper involvement with other people. My loving service would be my way of praying. I would find God in others, leaving behind this dreary struggle for a personal spiritual life (whatever that was, now that the early joy had gone out of it) and giving myself wholly to each person I met. Surely that would replenish me. It didn't, of course. Several years later I read Agnes Sanford's description of her missionary father:

> Very likely no one knew the cause of his collapse, referred to vaguely as a nervous breakdown. Looking back...I can see a cause they never saw: he was doing the work of the Holy Spirit without the full power of the Holy Spirit ....The healing of souls and the forgiveness of sins that Our Lord accomplished through my father were real and true. But since the wellspring of God's power had not been awakened in him, the toll on his own strength was great, and the nerves of his body could not stand it.[1]

This description fit me, except there was no nervous breakdown.

Instead, I experienced a dulling of my emotional responses; a dark savorlessness crept into my daily life.

I also experienced a significantly concurrent loss of my own identity as a minister. I found myself wondering what I was really doing. If I were there to help others on an outer level only, then any trained social worker, professional therapist, or expert community organizer could do the job more efficiently than I.

There were, of course, many genuine joys in my life at that time. My husband was always understanding and supportive (a backing that many Christian leaders do not have in their personal lives!) even when I could not clearly articulate the problem. I still enjoyed some aspects of church fellowship, the intellectual challenge of sermon preparation and classes, and the stimulation of ministry within a great city. *Outwardly* all appeared reasonably successful. But after some months of reflection, I decided to take a leave of absence from ministry that lasted seven years.

During that time, with my husband as full-time professor and with three children to care for, I was asking God to begin all over again with me. Help came in astonishingly varied ways and often from totally unexpected sources. It took me quite a while to realize that mere neglect of daily prayer was not the essential problem. It was a symptom. The real problem went much deeper.

Put simply, I had not understood what relationship with God really meant. I had not understood that some of my basic concepts about God needed healing. I did not understand at all the vital part that our bodily-emotional self plays in healthy spirituality. I did not understand the effect that unhealed wounds and communal toxicity and draining have on one's emotional and spiritual life. I did not know about the praying that *underlies* praying when one is too tired or overwrought to pray. I did not know about the vital springs that go much deeper than good resolutions and willpower.

I did not trust God with the "shadow side" of much of my unfaced, unacknowledged inner self. I had not realized that Jesus' primary mission was not to teach us a bigger and better prayer discipline but to enable us to bring the wholeness of ourselves into relationship with God.

Perhaps we can compare our problem of relationship with God to the problem of a spouse who loves but is basically ignorant of the essence of marriage, a covenant of deep daily intimacy that calls each to bring his or her wholeness into the relationship. Only then do the marriage partners grow into greater wholeness together. If those entering the covenant do not understand its meaning, eventually (symptomatically) the ability to communicate spontaneously together will die.

I am still learning and growing in this understanding of the covenant with God. One of the most important things I have learned is that our growing closeness with God was never intended to be a burden or one more task added to all the other tasks. Personal relationship with God was meant to remove the sense of burden and to infuse all tasks with new vitality.

Much has changed for ministers in recent decades. Most theological schools now offer at least one course on spirituality, though such courses often are not taught by a full-time faculty member as are the courses on Bible, homiletics, counseling, church history, Christian ethics, and liturgy. Various institutes of spirituality now offer pastors courses in spirituality and courses on the emotional health of clergy and other Christian leaders. Most denominations provide spiritual retreats on a regular basis and demonstrate far more practical concern for the well-being of Christian leaders. Spiritual direction is no longer an unexplored mystery for Protestant Christian leaders but has become a widespread practice.

Also there has been an astonishing, almost explosive proliferation of books and workshops on almost every aspect of spiritual growth and its relationship to communities, politics, social justice, ethnic relationships, global ecology. Increasingly mainline churches are making the spiritual quest a high priority. In my twenty-seven years in this specialized ministry of spiritual renewal, I have seen an incredible heightening of interest and enthusiasm.

For example, up to a decade ago our large theological bookstore that serves the many theological schools in the Bay Area of northern California kept its book section on spirituality in the basement level in an obscure corner at the remote end of a corridor. It was difficult to find it at all! But now this section has the largest and most prominent display in the whole store located on the main floor by the entrance. Most of the best-selling books come from that section.

Nevertheless, as I talk with pastors and lay leaders at retreats around the country, I am still hearing deep spiritual longing, hunger, and loneliness. Some of these leaders received their theological training when I did. They really never were taught the deep meaning of spirituality and relationship with God. Some are experiencing inner draining and fatigue and do not understand why prayer does not seem to help. Others feel an uneasy dichotomy between what they consider their duty to God and their own personal basic needs. Some feel anxious that any focus on spirituality may cancel out their concern for social justice and the pain of the world community. Others have experimented with many forms of spiritual methodology, but nothing takes root in a lasting way. Some are pushing themselves into a prayer discipline not suited to them personally because an admired leader has urged it.

In this book, I share only what has become personally true and helpful for me, as well as what I have observed to be helpful in the lives of many of the pastors, priests, educators, chaplains, and other Christian leaders I have known personally. We need to share our stories, our discoveries, our mistakes, our surprises, our "epiphanies" with one another. And as we share, we encourage and affirm one another's uniqueness within God. No two stories are exactly alike because each is, at core, a unique love story.

REFLECTION AND MEDITATION

(Remember to move through all the meditations very slowly. Stop at any point you choose for more thought and focus. If you feel uncomfortable, leave the meditation or change the wording and metaphors. If you would find it helpful, write down your thoughts during the process.)

You desire truth in the inward being (Psalm 51:6).

Make your body comfortable in any way best for you. You may choose to sit up straight or lean back; lie on the floor, a bed, or the grass; or walk around quietly. Become aware of the muscles in your face, jaw, and shoulders, and move them gently to release any tightness. Take a few slow, deep breaths without pushing or straining. Then let your breath become slow and light.

Picture or just think of God's nearness in whatever way is most natural: light enfolding you or gentle hands holding you or a great mountain or a deep calm lake holding up your body. You may wish to think of or picture Jesus. Or you may choose to focus on a word or phrase, such as *light of the world, release to God, the living Christ, peace,* or other words that come naturally to you.

It may be enough just to think of each breath you draw as breathing in God's love and Spirit. Or just rest and quietly breathe.

If and when you feel ready, think of a time in your life as a Christian leader when, like Mary, you were "weeping beside the tomb." The time may have been one of dryness and boredom, of acute inner desolation and pain, a period of inner loneliness and lostness. Or perhaps you were experiencing a time of general inner fatigue. It may have been one or all of these. Was this a recent experience? long ago? Or are you in such a place right now?

What were, or are, some of the symptoms? How did or does this inner fatigue affect your daily life? your relationships? your work as a Christian leader?

Begin asking inner questions. Can you begin to discern any underlying cause? Had there been any sudden or long-term personal or communal trauma or abusiveness? Did unhealed memories suddenly surface? What might have caused or contributed to your drain? In what ways do you set healthy borders and limits? What areas of your work seem confining and purposeless? Has personal prayer dropped out or become savorless? If no basic cause of desolation appears, don't push. It is enough just to begin asking questions.

In this reflection try to express your deepest feeling and need in the most honest, plain, blunt words you can. Don't try to be theologically correct. You may wish to write or draw your responses or express what you feel through bodily gestures.

You may wish to reread the first sixteen verses of John 20. Even as Mary wept while looking into the empty tomb, she saw two angels but did not recognize them as such. Also, though again she did not know it, the risen Jesus was standing there, close behind her.

What meaning does this passage have for you now or at the time of an earlier spiritual desolation? What or who came to help you or is helpful to you now? a special person? a special activity? a piece of music or art? some work with your hands? a special thought or a book? some word? Or did anything help you? Was the manner of help surprising?

If you are now in a place where neither the "angels" nor the risen Jesus is manifest, just rest quietly and breathe in the early-morning freshness and expectancy of that story. The risen Christ stands next to you, though the knowing of it may come later.

Take note of what is happening in your body. Do you sense any release of tightness? Or has more tightness crept in? Don't try to force any relaxation. Just quietly breathe the fresh air of that story through those muscles.

When you feel ready, stretch and lightly massage your face, hands, and wrists. Bring your meditation to a gentle close, giving yourself time for reentry into your usual interaction with others around you before you start moving around and talking.

2

The Heart
of
Christian
Spirituality

Jesus said to her, "Mary"
(John 20:16).

*T*HERE IS A LUMINOUSNESS about each of the Resurrection stories: the gathering dusk of the walk to Emmaus, the depth of night as Jesus joins his disciples in the locked room, the freshness of early morning by Lake Tiberias as Jesus cooks breakfast for his friends. Perhaps the most poignant of all is that dawn in the garden of the sepulcher when Mary, blinded by tears, speaks to the "gardener" who simply says her name, "Mary!"

To me, this encounter is the heart and core of Christian spirituality. Wendy Wright's reflections on our internalization of this story struck me:

> I was once at an intimate mass where this Gospel was the reading of the day....The presider opted to allow those gathered to share their personal reflections on the scene. We were to listen prayerfully to the text and to imagine ourselves in the place of Mary Magdalene hearing our own name called....The presider recalled feeling that it was too good to be true. Another worshiper identified with Mary's sense of the changed relationship....I remember feeling overwhelmed at being recognized and met in the depths of my grief. I/Mary has lost what was dearest in life....Yet when hope was gone, my name was called.
>
> This dimension of the Easter event is astonishing. If only we could really hear our name called in those parts of ourselves and our world where hopelessness holds fast.[1]

There is no substitute for being looked at directly and called by our name.

Some years ago I attended a reception honoring a famous bishop, known throughout the country for his challenging theological stance and his passion for social justice. When I was introduced, he shook my hand and murmured a courteous word or two in my direction, but his eyes never once met mine. He gazed restlessly past my shoulder at the crowd and the room. He did the same with each person he met. It seemed as if each person did not really exist for him.

But as we read of Jesus' encounters, we sense how he looks directly at each person as if he or she were the only one present, in spite of the pressing crowds. Whether encountering a priest, a child, a soldier, a woman, a fisherman, a tax collector, a sick person, a scheming person, a best friend, a challenging enemy, Jesus never views persons as objects, case studies, interruptions, or a means to an end. We get no sense of an impersonal distancing.

God may be more than personal (whatever that might be), but God cannot be less than personal. Any spirituality that depersonalizes God or ourselves usually will depersonalize us and our relationships.

One of the great turning points in my life came when I read the Jewish Hasidic spiritual leader and author Martin Buber and later met him. His supreme (and difficult) book *I and Thou* literally changed my life at a time when I was headed rapidly into impersonal, depersonalized ways of thinking about God and myself in the name of spirituality. This little book released me into the ultimate personhood of God who also calls us into personhood. This experience of personhood endows us with the power to experience other people and all living things as personal, never as objects or "its."

Even when we use symbols or metaphors for God that seem impersonal, such as light, water, wind, mighty fortress (the psalms are full of these images), it is with the full understanding that these symbols are undergirded, filled, and drenched with the intense, personal love of God.

Not everyone experiences God's direct personal closeness. Recently a dedicated young woman pastor, a minister for twelve years, whose life is full of love and faith, told me sadly that she cannot feel this closeness. She admits she has experienced some startling answers to prayer. "But why can't I feel God?" she asks. "Other people have mystical experiences. Why not I?" Christians could lift a great burden of guilt and anxiety from their own shoulders if they felt assured that this lack of feeling God's closeness did not denote unworthiness or lack of faith. Jesus was much more concerned about the full honesty of our whole selves with God and the transforming changes that occur within us as we deepen in trust toward God.

Surprisingly Jesus actually *said* little about prayer, though obviously his life was drenched with prayer. He gave the model of what we call the Lord's Prayer because his disciples pointedly asked for it. (See Luke 11:1-4.) I have never believed that Jesus meant us to stick rigidly to those particular words. I think rather that he was indicating with simplicity, dignity, and intimacy the various aspects of life that we can talk about with God. He did not come to teach us mystical experiences or systems of a disciplined prayer life. Many great religious teachers and spiritual systems have taught these ways, and many still do. We can become more sensitively aware of God's presence through many helpful ways. There are also many ways by which we can be helped to recognize the experiences of God we have already had without knowing it. The sense of God's presence is often an experience of such naturalness that it surprises us to realize what it was.

The growing sense of God's closeness comes in diverse ways, and this book explores some of them. But I believe the unique essence of Christianity comes in encountering the heart of God through Jesus the Christ. For Christians, Jesus is the human, personal face of God. He reveals the mystery of God in a way we can touch, embrace, and trust. When I study any religion, any theological or spiritual system, I ask myself, *Does this reflect the experience of God I receive through Jesus in its fullness of love, freedom, mercy, challenge, transformation, and warm personhood?* If not, then some dimension is lacking, no matter how beautiful and noble in other respects. I am not being shown the full heart of God.

Recently Christian leaders have debated whether Christianity is a religion *about* Jesus or the religion *of* Jesus. I have problems with both definitions.

A religion *about* Jesus externalizes him; it puts him "out there" as a sort of Superman model, an external master of perfection to whom we submit. This definition is a form of projected hero worship, which leads to a primary response of obedience, conformity, and guilt—without much deep inner change.

But I find the religion *of* Jesus equally unhelpful. This definition turns Jesus into a kindly elder brother, a role model, a teacher and guide. This interpretation invites me to share and imitate Jesus' way of living and worshiping. To me, this understanding is flat and savorless. The hundreds of inspiring spiritual leaders throughout history may indeed help me through their teaching, but they are not in direct, living relationship with me. They are not with me now. They do not call me by name. They do not transform me.

This debate is not new. The Athanasians, Arians, and Pelagians hammered it out in the fierce (and sometimes bloody) battles among them, using the vocabulary of the early centuries of Christianity.

I suggest a third alternative: Christianity is religion *through* Jesus. This option offers us neither an externalized hero to idolize nor a role model to imitate. It offers us a living connectedness, a relationship with the living Jesus through whom we experience God, ourselves, other people, and all of life in a transformed and enhanced way.

> Abide in me as I abide in you.
> Just as the branch cannot bear fruit by itself
> unless it abides in the vine,

neither can you unless you abide in me.
I am the vine, you are the branches.
Those who abide in me and I in them
bear much fruit (John 15:4-5).

The branch does not stand apart and worship the vine, nor does it try to imitate the vine or become a vine. It is organically connected with the vine and shares the vine's abundant life. Our relationship with Jesus, in which our own life is united with and encompassed by Jesus' incredible and radiantly expanded life, releases us to our true and deepest selves. At the same time, this relationship carries us to dimensions of experience that we never dreamed possible.

This does not mean that Jesus stands between us and a direct experience of God. Such a concept and image can cause confusion and create a stumbling block. Naturally we want to experience God directly without a go-between or mediator. But this is the main point: *Through* Jesus we do experience God directly in an intensified and heightened way.

Two analogies help me here. When we fall deeply in love, we experience all of life in a new and intensified way. Colors are brighter; music is more poignant; other people are dearer; we have more energy for daily tasks. We have entered this deepened life because of our love relationship with the other person. That other person is not mediating life to us or standing between us and our direct experience of life. Rather, our connectedness with the other enhances everything. We experience life directly, fully, and in a way we never would have known without this other person. I'm not talking about codependency with its mutual drain and constriction but mutual life enhancement.

Another analogy that helps me is one I heard or read somewhere many years ago. The nature of the sun, like God, is to shine upon and enliven the whole earth. The sun does not play favorites. But if one puts a magnifying glass in the rays of the sun over a pile of leaves, the light will turn into fire. We can compare Jesus the Christ to that magnifying glass held in God's light.

When we experience God's love through our connectedness with Jesus, we have moved under the magnifying glass. It is the same sun, the same light; but within the impact of that Christ personality, we experience that light as fire. The glass does not prevent us from a direct experience of the sun—it enormously enhances it.

For me, this direct enhancement is the Resurrection relationship. This enhanced relationship is what I mean when I pray in Jesus' name. In the biblical sense, a *name* denoted the living, unique reality of the person—the essence of the person. (In some cultures persons secretly guarded their real names for fear that an enemy could exert power over them by using it.)

We Christian leaders have the real handicap of speaking Jesus' name so often professionally that experiencing the impact of its intimate, awesome power can become difficult for us. But sometimes we break through those veils of common usage and discover again for ourselves its almost vibratory empowerment. When we use the name of Jesus, we have deliberately and intentionally put ourselves under the magnifying glass of his living personality. The fruit and the fire come into being.

Again, Christian leaders find it hard to talk or write this way since we know how often people will misinterpret and misunderstand. We know all too well how the name of Jesus is misused or abused: We have heard it used pietistically and sentimentally. We have heard it used manipulatively. We have heard it used punitively. We have heard it used as a political or ecclesiastical weapon. We have heard it used to build dividing walls. We have heard it used in ways that make us want to hide!

Twenty years ago I gathered a small group of women about my age. We met for discussion and sharing. All except one were ministers' spouses. Without exception they all told me that it made them acutely uncomfortable when I prayed in Jesus' name. They associated Jesus' name with emotional distancing (and sometimes emotional abuse) from their spouses—and also with rigid church members and church practices. That name seemed to stand between them and their full freedom and self-value as persons.

Two daughters of a dear friend were deeply involved in a small cult for many years (though it called itself a church). An appallingly abusive and dominating woman led the cult. She directed the cult members' every act and thought: how they would relate to their spouses and their children; whether they should go to a doctor; whether they should attend university; what movies and T.V. shows they could watch; what jobs they should take; how they should pray, think, talk, play. She used the Bible as a club. She would call members forward for public rebuke and shaming. She would quote Bible verses at them and tell them how angry Jesus was with them. The two girls managed to extricate themselves from this cult several years ago, but to this day attending any church service, even for a funeral or wedding, literally terrifies them. The Bible for them is still a source of fear and guilt. For them the name of Jesus is a throwback into an atmosphere of punishment and condemnation.

I still recall the acute embarrassment I felt as a university sophomore in my first speech class. Our first assignment was to give a five-minute speech. One student used his five minutes to deliver a fervid evangelical sermon on how to be saved by Jesus. Never before had the use of the beloved name of Jesus given me such pain and anger! Before a captive audience, required to sit in silence and hear one another's speeches, the student chose to use Jesus' name inappropriately and manipulatively. This secular university included members from other religions. Though I was a fellow-Christian with a call into ministry, I was ashamed of him. This was religious assault!

But these episodes are mild compared to the countless times in Christian history when Jewish community members were forced into Christian churches and made to hear sermons in the name of Jesus that attacked them and their faith! One of the great tragedies of history is that the name intended to set us free, to bring us into wholeness, to transform us through love has been the impetus for manipulation and coercion against so many.

Yet somehow the loving, transforming power of Jesus' name rises again from the worst we can do to it, just as the living Jesus rose from the grave. Without this relationship of the believer to the living Christ, Christianity may be a faith of noble ideas and ideals, but it will have lost its wind, fire, salt, and yeast.

Personal encounters with the risen Jesus pulled the disciples out of their pit of grief, shock, and despair after the crucifixion. The disciples were not (I am reasonably sure) sitting on a panel discussion, working on a new communal movement that they would metaphorically entitle "Resurrection." Jesus' coming to them startled the disciples beyond words. They saw him, touched him, heard him. It does not matter whether what they saw was an actual physical body, a spiritual body manifested in physical form, or a merging and intermingling of the two. (After all, what is physical matter except a form of invisible energy?) The point is this: The disciples had a personal encounter through which they experienced the full impact of Jesus' unique personhood.

Millions have experienced a similar impact up to this present time. The two covers of the Bible cannot confine Jesus. Somewhere Martin Luther referred to the scriptures as the cradle of the Eternal Word. "He is there found, but is not there confined" is another magnificent saying whose source I have forgotten.

This inability to confine Jesus frightens some Christians. Recently when I led a retreat for a fairly conservative branch of the church, a group of six members (out of a hundred or more attending) called me into a private caucus and accused me of releasing demonic forces into the community! The main problem stemmed from my references to Jesus' ongoing presence and work with us without citing a specific Bible verse each time. I reminded the group that John's Gospel concludes with the words: "But there are also many other things that Jesus did;

if every one of them were written down, I suppose that the world itself could not contain the books that would be written" (John 21:25). I asked the members if they really believed that Jesus' acts and words stopped with the last word in the Book of Revelation? Was it not just the beginning?

I reminded the group members that while we owe accountability to the scriptures and their basic vision and meaning, they are our touchstone, not a confining prison of the living truth. They listened politely (though I am not sure they *heard* me) but did not change their opinion that I was inspired by the devil. The next day the six left the retreat and returned home.

I have seldom had this experience personally, but I am concerned that many branches of the church have a growing suspicion and fear of the belief that Jesus cannot be pinned down and structured into safe categories.

At the other extreme, we see branches of the church that believe Jesus is only a "memory in the mind of God." Any talk of an ongoing relationship threatens these members, creating fear in them: fear of idolatry, fear of superstition, fear of pietism. Some mainline churches seem almost embarrassed by Jesus.

Unfortunately, actual personal encounters with the living Christ are one of the best-kept secrets in our Christian communities. But thousands through the ages have seen him in their waking state or have heard his voice or felt his touch. Many more—though not actually hearing or seeing or feeling—have experienced his vivid, unmistakable presence. Perhaps even more of us have not *felt* anything but have experienced a miraculous personal transformation in our lives when we have called on the name of Jesus.

Morton Kelsey, Episcopal priest, Jungian scholar, spiritual leader, and author of many of the most intelligent and perceptive books on spirituality in this generation, writes,

> At an ecumenical conference of some two hundred people, I invited the attendees to write down their most important

religious experiences and share them with me. Fully half of the fifty accounts I received described the appearance of Christ—indeed, this was the most significant part of their experience.[2]

Repeatedly pastors, theological students, chaplains, teachers, lay leaders have described their personal experiences with the risen Jesus to me. During my years as pastor, I would have found these experiences incomprehensible, despite the fact that as a teenager I had felt called into ministry because of such an experience. Somehow I had pushed that experience into the back of my mind and memory as a sort of metaphorical illusion.

Again it is vitally important to emphasize that though these direct experiences of Jesus' presence are widespread, they are *not* the necessary qualification for faith, ministry, or even daily life abiding in the risen Jesus. "Blessed are those who have not seen and yet have come to believe," Jesus said the week after his Resurrection to Thomas (John 20:29). They are blessed, which means both happy and energized, because the transforming full-life encounter can happen whether we see the presence or not.

It is enough to affirm Jesus' living presence at work in our lives, to call on the power of the Risen One, to pray in Jesus' name, to ask the living Jesus to enfold our lives with his transcendent life. It is enough to picture or to think of Jesus looking directly at us and speaking our name as those who are personally loved and loved forever. It is enough to grow in the trust that enables us to tell "him the whole truth," as the hemorrhaging woman did. (See Mark 5:33.)

When this encounter happens, each one of us becomes a new and miracle-filled Book of Acts.

REFLECTION AND MEDITATION

I have called you by name, you are mine (Isa. 43:1).

Rest your body in whatever way is best for you. Breathe a few slow full breaths, then let your breathing become light and gentle. You may wish to imagine an inward picture or to say a few words that help you feel God's closeness.

When you feel ready, focus your thoughts on the biblical Jesus. Bring to mind a special story of an encounter with Jesus: Jesus' laying healing hands on someone, blessing the children, walking by the lake with the disciples, calling forth Lazarus, waking up Jairus's little girl, sailing on the lake, eating supper with his disciples, speaking to Mary in the garden, or any other story. Think about the story for a while, letting it become lovingly real for you.

Now think of or picture yourself as one of the persons in that story, perhaps the person being healed or spoken to or touched. Let yourself feel or think of Jesus' direct personal attention; sense the direct gaze of his eyes. Remember he came not to condemn but to make us whole.

What are you experiencing about God that is clarified and intensified for you through this meeting with Jesus?

You may prefer to think of Jesus now in our time, beside you. It does not matter if you cannot picture his face or clothes. Just think of the direct encounter with Jesus. Envision that distinct, empowered personality looking at you, talking with you, taking your hand.

You may choose to recall a past experience you have had with Jesus. Remember it now. What about that particular experience made you know it was Jesus? What did you learn about God through this encounter?

Or you may wish just to say Jesus' name. You might want to say it with the Aramaic pronunciation, *Yeshua* (YEH-shoe-ah), to give it a fresh, new sound. Remember that when you call on the name, you call on the person's essence, the deep personal reality.

Or you might wish to say a short, powerful invocation, such as: "In the Name, by the Word, and in the Light of Jesus Christ."

When you feel ready, think of Jesus' question to Peter: "But who do *you* say that I am?" (Matt. 16:15, *italics mine*). Let this be a personal question to you. What rises from your heart? Try *not* to give a well-articulated, theologically correct response. No one is listening to you except Jesus. Let your response be honest, whether expressed through a word, a cry, a shrug, a longing, a bodily gesture, or another way.

Move deeper now than just words, ideas, or inner pictures. Rest in the presence that is with you, whether you feel anything special or not.

You may wish to meditate on these words of Teilhard de Chardin:

> Now grace is the sap which, rising in the one trunk, spreads through all the veins in obedience to the pulsations of the one heart....and the radiant Head, the mighty Heart, the fruitful Tree are, of necessity, Christ.[3]

What do you feel you are learning about and experiencing of God through this luminosity of the living Jesus Christ?

When ready, conclude your meditation, stretch, and lightly massage your face and hands. Take a few more quiet moments before you return to your usual interactions.

3

Spiritual Release or Spiritual Abuse?

The doors…were locked…Jesus came and stood among them (John 20:19).

E CAN PICTURE THE DISCIPLES that Easter night, meeting secretly behind the locked doors. Strange rumors are circulating. Jesus has reportedly been seen alive. Is this a trap set by the authorities to catch them? Has an ambitious impostor arrived on the scene who will get them all in trouble?

Even if it is Jesus, it is far safer to meet behind locked doors. Perhaps some of them feel secretly that it is better to lock the doors *especially* if it is Jesus! They have let him down badly in Gethsemane, at his trial, at his death. If it is really he, what will he say to them? Can they bear it? These future shepherds of the church are afraid, ashamed, and traumatized.

Then quietly Jesus comes and stands among them. He does not stand outside the locked door, knocking. Nor does he break down the door. Nor does he go away, offended at their fear.

This story shows the love of God that honors the choice to lock a door, the love that will not force a door but whose love cannot be barred out by a door. That love came through gently with power. Genuine power is the opposite of force. The love stood among them without reproach. The love spoke *shalom*, the peace that translates as "well-being" and "wholeness," in the very midst of their dark fear and shame. The love was with them, sharing wounds and vulnerability; the love breathed the empowering Spirit upon them. In this story we see a love that is pervasive without being invasive.

The next week the disciples gather again; they lock the door again. We might have thought that having once experienced the

Resurrection reality, they would never need to lock a door again. But most of us understand; we ourselves have locked the door more than twice. Again the love comes through. Jesus invites Thomas to put out his finger and see the wounds there, then to put out his whole hand and touch the wounds. What a merciful way to call oneself or another into relationship—by gradual stages: first to look, then to touch, then to enter covenant. Nothing is forced; nothing is rushed; no one is condemned.

This marvelous paradigm reminds us that God enters our hidden places of darkness, wound, fear, and doubt with gentleness. Yet many abusive forms of spirituality surround us. I have open before me a well-known book on spiritual guidance in which the author explains step by step how to pronounce the sentence of death upon one's natural self, upon one's ego, and then how to carry out the execution. Also here on my desk is a suggested liturgy, a responsive reading in which we ask God to increase and sharpen our fears, hurts, shame, and doubt until we reach such a pinnacle of pain that we finally break loose from our inner blocks. As I read this prayer, I am thinking of a marriage I observed recently in which the husband deliberately teased, mocked, and prodded his wife's most painful vulnerabilities, knowing exactly which buttons to push to "teach her a lesson" and to push her past her "immaturities." In human relationships, we call this verbal abuse.

I love most of George Matheson's (1842–1906) hymns, but one he wrote appalls me:

> Make me a captive, Lord, and then I shall be free.
> Force me to render up my sword, and I shall conqueror be.
> I sink in life's alarms, when by myself I stand;
> imprison me within thine arms, and strong shall be my hand.
> My heart is weak and poor until it master find;
> it has no spring of action sure, it varies with the wind.
> It cannot freely move, till thou has wrought its chain;
> enslave it with thy matchless love, and deathless it shall reign.

This is such fascinating, powerful imagery—and such dangerous theology! What would we say of a marriage or any relationship that waxed enthusiastic about force, captivity, imprisonment, chains, enslavement? We know what we would call that manner of relationship—and it has an ugly name!

The fact that Matheson makes this plea for the sake of inner spiritual freedom makes the imagery not better but worse. God through Jesus relates to us with a freedom that sets us free. Matheson's hymn does not reflect the Resurrection relationship or the divine-human marriage feast. It implies violation!

Nothing in our bonding with Jesus forces us "to render up our sword." Obviously God offers us a better way than the sword, and God longs for us to grow into the power of the better way. But Jesus permitted the disciples to bring swords with them to Gethsemane the night of the betrayal. (See Luke 22:36, 38.) He did not allow them to draw the sword for *him*, but he permitted the disciples to use the swords in their own defense if they chose. He knew the day would come when they would no longer need or choose that way of outer defense, but he never forced them to choose that way then—nor does he now.

Whatever the "sword" may be in our own lives—our defensiveness, our fearful confrontations, our body armor, our emotional fortress, our walls and masks—our sword came into being in our earlier days of vulnerability when our trust was threatened or abused. These masks that hide our true feelings, these walls that divide us from others and our own deep selves, these inner doors that lock out intimacy: They are our tears and wounded flesh masquerading as swords—as masks, walls, and doors. The healing that God brings through Jesus does not tear off masks or knock down doors. God is not a destroyer but a more radical Spirit who works and creates from our deepest roots.

I believe we use so much assaulting spiritual language and methodology for two reasons. One is the hierarchical spiritual structure we have projected upon the Christian relationship, which is not in accordance with Jesus' covenant with us:

"No longer do I call you servants,
for the servant does not know what the master is doing;
but I have called you friends,
for all that I have heard from my Father I have made known
to you" (John 15:15).

If we took that covenant of Jesus seriously, we would stop thinking of ourselves primarily as God's servants. We would move
out of the realm of master-servant, dominance-submission,
conquest-surrender. We would experience voluntary *self*-render
(a giving *to*), not *sur*render (a giving *up* to). Our free giving of
ourselves would bring us into intimate bonding with God, into
that spontaneous grace in which those who love do indeed
serve one another, not as servants but as lovers. Jesus' covenant
emphasizes the bondedness not the bondage, the covenant not
the obedience, the communion not the submission. We would
not do things so much *for* God as *with* God and *within* God.

Then why does Jesus say in that same passage: "This is my
commandment, that you love one another," and "You are my
friends if you do what I command you" (John 15:12, 14). What
paradox is this? Can one *command* one's beloved friends? Can
one command love? Do his words put us back into the master-
slave way of relating?

I looked up the root meaning of the word *command*. Its
Latin roots refer to *mandate*, the giving of a delegated represen-
tative power into the hand of another person. Politically, for
example, a viceroy is the legal, implicit presence of the sovereign
who delegates. An ambassador and an embassy are the legal
presence of the country they represent.

The Greek roots of *command* also mean authorization. It is
fascinating that another one of the root meanings in Greek
refers to the enabling of something new coming into being!

Therefore the basic meaning of command is not an act of
disempowering another. It refers to the use of power placed
into one's hand in the name of the one who delegates, backed
by the full power of the delegator.

I recall a significant incident in the winter of 1989–90 when so many Communist governments were collapsing in eastern Europe. In one of those countries a political fugitive fled as far as the fence of the West German Embassy. The police were about to seize him when a staff member (not an important one) of that embassy ran out through the gate, wrapped his arm and his coat around the fugitive, and led him through the gate onto the embassy grounds. Legally, so long as the staff member held onto the fugitive, that person was safe. No one could touch the fugitive because at that moment this staff member embodied the whole "command" of that embassy's country. For those few minutes, the staff member *was* his country, empowered by its full authority.

So when Jesus "commands" us in the name of love to act with love, it is an empowerment given into our hand. We are not acting just on our own responsibility but are backed by the full meaning and presence of God. We do not so much represent God as actually embody God's heart at that moment and in that situation.

The difference, of course, between a legal mandate and God's mandate is that God's love, experienced through Jesus, is not a legalistic matter. We are not just a means to an end. We are not "instruments" of God's will. We are the beloved. God's mandate, God's empowerment in us and through us is a sacramental act that brings blessing upon the one who acts and the one acted upon. It is akin to the marriage union (a frequent biblical metaphor) in which the lovers confer God's sacramental power upon each other. Lovers do not so much surrender to each other, but rather both give themselves, render themselves, to the love that unites them.

Ron DelBene expresses with clarity and power the love-drenched nature of God's mandate:

> Unfortunately, many people view the will of God as rather like a ten-ton elephant hanging overhead, ready to fall on

them if they don't make the right decision. Actually, the word which we translate into English as *will* comes from both a Hebrew and a Greek word which mean "yearning." It is the yearning which lovers have for one another.[1]

Spiritual abusiveness may arise if we focus on the structures of religion rather than on the freedom of relationship with the beloved. Obviously we need structure and order, an articulate theological, ecclesiastical, and liturgical framework—just as a family living together in love needs a dwelling place that won't collapse, a budget, housekeeping agreements, shared responsibilities, and family traditions. But the deadly temptation is to identify the order and structure with the wellspring of the love that drew these people together in the first place. If we permit the unique, personal relationship to become dulled and superseded by structural details, the spirit of the communal body (whether family, church, or nation) begins to sleep, and eventually to die.

The relationship, not the rules, builds the strength of the inner life. From the relationship, not the rules, healing takes place and transformation happens. I often use with delight a quote that I read somewhere, which explained that the Sermon on the Mount was not *prescriptive* but *descriptive*. Jesus was not just handing out orders but describing what begins to happen spontaneously when we are in living relationship with the source of life. We begin to change at the root. For example, we find it increasingly natural to pray for rather than curse an enemy. The mandate, the conferred empowerment to become the embodiment of God's love, flows into our bloodstream, our lifestream, our very core.

The distinction between the structures of religion and the spontaneity of relationship is expressed with concise power in the autobiography of Patricia Nolan Savas:

> *Religion* is "I have to."
> *Relationship* is "I want to."

Religion is the parable for the world to read.
Relationship speaks plainly to the listening, watchful heart.

Religion requires outward signs or symbols.
Relationship offers, "Come, let me introduce you
    to the living reality behind these symbols."...

Religion is an obligation, often resulting in guilt and anxiety.
Relationship is an adventure, producing joy and wonder....

Religion is the schoolteacher telling about God.
Relationship is experiencing God....

Religion does things for God.
Relationship abides in God.

Religion is the shadow or blueprint of the real thing.
Relationship **is** the real thing.[2]

I believe that any form of spirituality that tempts us to shift the priority of relationship with God to a prioritized structure with obedience, submission and conformity as its characteristics is not the spirituality of Jesus Christ. We can discern this shift within ourselves by asking these questions about leaders, books, prayer groups, institutes, spiritual directors, or spiritual programs:

- Is my freedom within this process respected? Am I free to withdraw, withhold, keep silence if I choose?

- Are my human needs and feelings respected? Am I encouraged to say what I feel, or am I made to feel guilty and unspiritual if I express feelings and needs?

- Is my own inner timing respected? Am I hurried into premature and programmed responses? Am I given space to reflect and come to my own conclusions and decisions in my own time?

- Do I feel free to ask questions, to disagree, to express ambivalence and ambiguity? Do I feel listened to and heard when I express dissent and uncertainty?

- Am I encouraged with this person or within this system to listen to and trust my instincts and inner guidance, or am I increasingly led to distrust myself? Am I urged, or is it implied, that I should trust only this leader, this group, this system?

• Do I feel valued and respected as a unique human being beloved by God even if I withdraw from this group or this system?

Anything that returns us to inner prisons of the spirit (no matter how holy it seems), back behind the dividing walls (whether inner or outer), back into denial of the whole self is not of Jesus Christ, even if using his name—and thus abusing his name.

Certain forms of spirituality often have perverted the basic uses of self-denial into *denial of the self*, thereby avoiding the full truth about one's whole self: one's wounds, powers, needs, gifts—the shadow side as well as the overt side. Sheila, Dennis, and Matthew Linn reflect on the addictive forms of religion that can arise when we refuse to encounter our full selves:

> I've learned that an addiction is any substance or process we use to escape from and get control over a painful reality in our lives, especially painful feelings....It has become clear to me that we can use religion or religious things in exactly the same way as drugs or alcohol, to escape from what is real within....Religious addiction attempts to control painful inner reality through a religious belief system....
>
> Religion is often taught as a system of control, of rules, of rituals, of ideals, of shoulds. It's very easy to use all this to squelch the process of life, all the while thinking we're being good Christians. Shame-based people are particularly vulnerable to this, having been raised in a way that taught them not to trust themselves.[3]

As we grow into this freedom of facing both the pain and the power of our whole selves and learn to love our own humanness, we enter into full relationship with God rather than simply relating to belief systems about God. This growth requires great gentleness both toward ourselves as well as others.

A second reason we sometimes use spiritually abusive language and methodology relates to our desperate longing to grow, to move, to change. We weary of our inner traps and spiritual prisons, the fears that cripple us, the inertia that holds us back. We begin to think that nothing but force can change us and others.

Let us reread and reflect again upon the supreme stages of trust building, healing, and transformation behind those locked doors that Easter night.

So often we Christian leaders in our enthusiasm (especially when we ourselves begin to experience deep healing and growth) try to impose our agendas on those we lead. We urge everyone to enter into our prayer methodology; to participate in innovative worship, spiritual dancing, communal back rubs, public sharing ("Turn to the person next to you and share what you are thinking and feeling"), and guided meditations without explicit permission to abstain, withdraw, or keep silent.

We assume (incorrectly) that if people feel uncomfortable with our suggestion, they will simply not do it. But most people are frighteningly obedient (even ministers!) when guided by respected leaders. This obedience is especially dangerous when we work in the area of deep inner wounds of unhealed memories and the closed-off areas of hidden anger, fear, and shame. This is hot and holy ground! We can approach it safely only with utmost respect and gentleness.

When we lead a prayer group, a retreat, a healing group, an innovative worship service, a person in spiritual direction, we need to practice the "released" approach by giving explicit permission every time for any participant to keep silent, to withdraw from the process or activity, to change the metaphors and imagery, to do anything necessary to feel safe. If we do not respect the inner timing of the healing and trust-forming process, we may do extreme harm to the bruised spirit and the frightened heart.

A good way for Christian leaders to practice the released rather than the "invasive" approach is to observe when we are becoming invasive towards ourselves (times when we choose to ignore our own inner resistances). Earlier, I suggested questions we may ask about leaders and systems of spirituality. An equally important spiritual awareness is *listening* to our own inner resistances and asking what they are trying to tell us about our own walls and masks.

When I am aware of inner withdrawal or sense a mask forming over my spontaneity or experience a feeling of discomfort or a desire to attack, I am learning to ask myself in the presence of the Christ, "Who and what are these resistances?" I try to honor their presence, knowing they developed at some point of my vulnerability when I felt I needed protection. I am learning to question these feelings of resistance: "Why are you here? Are you reminding me of some wound of trust? Are you pointing to some unnamed fear behind a locked door? Are you telling me that I feel rushed or pushed by the people around me? Are you telling me I need more space, more time than I am giving myself? Are you a sign of some inner guidance that I have not recognized?"

If we learn to respect our inner resistances and learn to listen to them, we become increasingly sensitive to the real but often unspoken resistances of others. If we are gentle with our own growth process, we become gentle and respectful to the differing growth processes of others.

Gentleness is not weakness. It is not inertia. It is not an "anything goes" attitude. It is a tremendous power. Gentleness is not the same as denial of reality. It is a truth teller that speaks "the truth in love" (Eph. 4:15). It does not assault or violate the victim with more truth than he or she can bear at that moment. It speaks with the powerful gentleness of Jesus' talking to his disciples that last night before his death: "I still have many things to say to you, but you cannot bear them now" (John 16:12).

If we panic, thinking that we will never grow, never change, we need to remind ourselves that we have been trapped in our inner prisons for so long because we have not taken the time to listen to and understand our pain and resistance. Perhaps we have tried to use force rather than inviting the living Christ to enter our locked rooms with the love that does not force but transforms. A wise teacher once said to me, "Jesus Christ meets us fully where we are—but does not leave us there."

The words of a poignant Easter hymn describe the gentle but inexorable rising of Christ's transforming life within us:

Now the green blade riseth from the buried grain,
Wheat that in the dark earth many days has lain;
Love lives again, that with the dead has been:
Love is come again, like wheat that springeth green.
                   —John Macleod Campbell Crum (1872–1958)

When I compare this hymn to the Matheson hymn with its force, chains, and captivity, I see so fully the difference between the spirituality that releases and the spirituality that assaults. Whenever I am tempted to rush or push myself or another into any decision or process of growth, I try to remember the green blade's rising from the buried grain, responding to the life so much deeper and radically empowering than my own vision and will. For God is the lover, not the invader.

REFLECTION AND MEDITATION

Jesus came and stood among them and said,
"Peace be with you" (John 20:19).

Rest your body in whatever way feels best. Breathe a few slow, deep breaths; then let your breath become light and gentle. Think of the enfolding love of God through Jesus close in the room with you. Use an inner picture or inner words that help make this presence real for you. Take all the time you need to rest in this presence, knowing you are fully understood and fully loved forever.

When and if you feel ready, think of some part of yourself that feels locked up, closed, walled off; something in you that feels very vulnerable, something that does not want to be touched, interfered with, or brought out into the open. You may know what this is. Perhaps you do not clearly understand what it is that wants to hide out of sight. Perhaps it manifests its presence through tight muscles in your jaw, face, shoulders, hands, or abdomen. Do not try to do anything forcibly about this inner vulnerable area. At this point, don't even try to analyze it. Just quietly note the existence of a closed-off place within you that you prefer not to be opened.

If you become aware of deep fear and resistance, claim the love of God—allow the light of Christ gently to enfold this inner fear like a womb around the baby or a cocoon around the chrysalis. If you don't even want the feeling of being enfolded, you may wish only to think of or to picture a soft light glowing *outside* your inner door. Then leave the meditation at this time. You may wish to come back to it later. You may wish to talk about how you feel with trusted friends or with a spiritual counselor or therapist.

But if you feel safe and wish to proceed, first sense or picture the healing light outside your closed door; then think of the healing presence *inside* the door. But nothing is broken down or torn away. Christ the Comforter is there on the inside with your fear. Your fear is not alone in the dark.

Just rest and breathe in the presence that does not condemn. If such a gesture feels natural to you, consider laying your hand on a tight body part. Amazingly, the release of tightness in a body muscle can flow inward to the corresponding emotion.

When you feel ready, think of Jesus' words to the disciples, "Peace [*shalom*] be with you" (John 20:19).

Focus on the word *peace*. It means wholeness and well-being. The presence of the living Christ is speaking and breathing well-being and wholeness in the very center of your fear, your vulnerable place. Stay in this living presence of the shalom as long as it feels right for you. Let your vulnerable, defended place breathe it in.

This may be enough for you at this time. If so, move out of the meditation when it feels right. But if you wish to go on, focus on the words: "He breathed on them and said to them 'Receive the Holy Spirit'" (John 20:22).

If you are not comfortable with inner pictures, just repeat the words inwardly and reflect on their profound meaning. Even though the doors still were locked for fear, even though the disciples had not yet responded to Jesus' presence with touch or commitment; nevertheless, the empowerment of the Holy Spirit was breathed upon them. We not only are loved in the midst of our vulnerability and fear, we also are empowered in the heart of that closed-off inner room. The transformation has begun before we have done a thing!

Take all the time you need to breathe in not only that presence but also that Strength that trusts you even in the midst of your fear.

When you feel ready, move on to the words: "Put your finger here and see" (John 20:27). Say them slowly, inwardly.

What do these words say to you, where you are now? Is your inner bruised vulnerability ready to put out a finger just to see? Are you feeling able at this point to move closer to that presence and light?

How would you respond if instead the presence of Christ were to touch *you* very gently where you feel the most bruised and withdrawn?

When ready (and only if ready), move on to the next words: "Reach out your hand and put it in my side" (John 20:27). Again inwardly say these words slowly. God is sharing God's own vulnerability with you. We are not forced or hurried. What does this verse mean to you at this time?

The "whole-hand" response may come much later. Let your trust grow according to your own need and rhythm of response. You don't need to do everything in this first meditation. You may come back to it as often as you wish.

Think about the closed door or the inner wall or inner

mask. Think or picture the Christ laying healing hands upon the door, wall, or mask. This healing touch may not manifest itself outwardly for a long time, but the change has begun inwardly, at your very center.

When ready, close your meditation with stretching and light massage of your face and hands. As you give yourself a few moments of quietness before talking, remind yourself that Christ's glowing presence still radiates in your inner room, behind your doors, even when you are not thinking about it.

You may want to write down your experience with this trust-building meditation and later discuss your experience with a friend or spiritual guide. Be sure that the person with whom you talk understands the dynamics of a trust-building process and the need to respect the wounds that lie behind the walls.

You may choose to return often to this meditation, taking special note of any changes within your body, your feelings, and any new spontaneous images or words that rise within you.

Incarnational Spirituality

"Touch me and see"
(Luke 24:39).

HERE IS ALMOST A FEELING of hearty, delighted laughter in Luke's account of Jesus among his disciples that Easter night. Jesus assures them he is not a ghost. He asks them for something to eat (anything lying around will do!) and demonstrates his ability both to chew and swallow the bread and fish. Whatever this mysterious intermingling and merging of flesh and spirit, Jesus demonstrates it is really he—the person they have known and loved, completely recognizable. Perhaps this was the only way he could swiftly convince them in a manner they could grasp: by eating the types of foods they had shared so often and eating it in front of them.

A skeptic of a generation ago responded to a friend's description of his father's appearing to him after death formally dressed for the opera by saying, "I'm sorry, but I don't believe in the immortality of top hats!"

The skeptic missed the point, of course. The hat was a recognizable symbol of the father's surviving personality, his actual presence. It was a bodily connecting link that his son would recognize immediately. The hat was not immortal, but the father's identity and sense of humor were.

Jesus did not come to his friends as a ghostly, ethereal mist, speaking mystical words. He came to them as himself in a way they could recognize, see, hug, speak to, eat with.

The surprising materiality of the Gospels can be a stumbling block to some of us. In my early ministry, I was thankful that my denomination did not (at that time) focus on the lectionary. By preaching on passages of my own selection, I could avoid all

those embarrassing parts of the synoptic Gospels: bodily heal-
ings, casting out of demons, feeding crowds from a few pieces
of bread and fish, turning water into wine, and so on. I could
focus on the Gospel stories that I considered to be more spiritual. In those days I still believed that spiritual growth would
make me detached, imperturbable. I would transcend my bodily-
emotional self, which would quietly fold up and drift away.

It was not that I thought my bodily self was in itself sinful,
despicable, or unworthy. Having been brought up in a liberal
church, on the whole I respected the bodily existence. I had
laughed (and still do) at the story of the sixteenth-century
Huguenot general who contemptuously noted his hands shaking with fatigue as he shaved before riding out to battle.
"Tremblest thou, vile carcass?" he sneered at his reflection in the
mirror. "Thou would'st tremble even more if thou knewest
where I will take thee this day!"

But I had assumed that our materiality was a condition at
least somewhat lower on the spiritual hierarchy scale. Certainly
many faiths and philosophies even that predate Christianity
taught the concept that we are to surmount our bodies as well
as our human personalities and human emotions. Such phrases
as "imprisoned splendor" were lodged into my attitudes as I
thought of the body-soul connection. Our bodily-emotional
selves are constrictions to the spirit in our assumptions. Though
not taught by Jesus or by orthodox Judaism, this subtle demot-
ing attitude toward our embodiment has crept into the deep
consciousness of most branches of the Christian faith.

Even the word *spiritual* can become a stumbling block for
many of us. Close your eyes and ask yourself this question:
What images leap to mind when I hear the word spiritual? Ask a
group to do this and then invite participants to share their first
spontaneous associations with that word. Most of the first
impressions will reflect a condition that is bodiless and basically
detached from earthly emotions.

But in the last several decades, there *have* been some deep changes in much spiritual teaching about our embodiment as we learn more about the mysterious interweaving of our physical, emotional, and spiritual health. We have become increasingly aware that our physical bodies are not impersonal machines to be dealt with mechanically. Our bodies are vibratory manifestations of the spirit, just as matter is a form of energy perceptible to our five senses.

The words of Teilhard de Chardin, French Jesuit, paleontologist, and spiritual leader, thrilled many of us when his book *Hymne de l'Univers* (*Hymn of the Universe*) was first published in 1961. He speaks as God's voice to the human being:

> "You hoped that the more thoroughly you rejected the tangible, the closer you would be to spirit; that you would be more divine if you lived in the world of pure thought, or at least more angelic if you had fled the corporeal? Well, you were like to have perished of hunger....
>
> "Purity does not lie in separation from, but in a deeper penetration into the universe....
>
> "Oh, the beauty of spirit as it rises up adorned with all the riches of the earth!"[1]

Recently many of us have become increasingly and excitedly aware of the witness and writings of those great medieval spiritual guides of the twelfth, thirteenth, and fourteenth centuries: Julian of Norwich, Mechtild of Magdeburg, and Hildegard of Bingen. With almost incredible power, they celebrated the beauty and spirituality of the material universe and our embodied selves when permeated with God's spirit. And going back as far as the fourth century, we find Saint John Chrysostom, patriarch in Constantinople, saying (ascetic though he was),

> Not for that we would be unclothed, but clothed upon, that mortality might be swallowed up in life. These are words by which the slanderers of the nature of the body, the impeachers of our flesh, are completely overthrown....We do not wish to cast aside the body, but corruption; not

flesh, but death ....What is foreign to us is not the body but corruptibility.[2]

Obviously—except why was it so unobvious to so many of us Christians for so many centuries?—this witness and celebration is profoundly scriptural. From Genesis to Revelation, scripture clearly affirms that the material world and ourselves as embodied beings are springing from the heart and will of God. The Apostle Paul sums it up quite simply:

> Do you not know that your body is a temple of the Holy Spirit within you...? Therefore glorify God in your body (1 Cor. 6:19, 20).

When Paul contrasts the works of the flesh with the works of the spirit (Gal. 5:16-21), he is not speaking of our physical embodiment as such. Since he includes in "works of the flesh" such things as idolatry, enmity, jealousy, party-spirit, clearly by "flesh" he means the unreconciled, abusive parts of our whole personalities, not the body.

The natural world was meant eventually to be a perfect manifestation of God's radiant love. In the vision of scripture, the pain, ruthlessness, and competitiveness of the natural world and our embodied condition will be transformed. (See Isa. 11; Rom. 8:19-21.)

In other words, to return to our Resurrection narratives, for a spiritual being raised from the dead to eat the bread and fish of life is perfectly natural. What is more, our eating of the bread and fish in our predeath bodies can be an act totally imbued with spirit. Isn't this part of the meaning of the sacramental words at Communion—"This is my body....This is my blood"—as we lift the bread and wine?

However, giving theological assent to the holiness of our embodiment is one thing; celebrating our own personal bodies is quite another. Not only do we Christian leaders have ambivalent feelings about our bodies, but certainly we find widespread anguish about embodiment among those to whom we minister.

Most ministers and other Christian leaders soon discover that detachment, fear, suspicion, and even hatred toward one's body stem from more than just bad theology. Such feelings are far more likely to find their roots in shame-filled, humiliating, abusive experiences. If persons come to us with serious eating disorders, sexual promiscuity or sexual repugnance, or any other form of bodily neglect and abuse, it is both ineffective and insensitive to enthuse over the holy beauty of the material world and their own bodies in particular. We need (gently) to inquire into the possibility of unfaced and unhealed emotional or physical abuse in their personal history. Their behaviors and attitudes may come from severe physical and emotional punishments and emotional deprivations during childhood. Or their problems may find their roots in childhood sexual abuse. These behaviors and attitudes can also develop during the adolescent years when teenagers often feel inferior or lacking in the cultural norms of beauty, skill, and stamina.

Abusive marriages or abusive adult sexual relationships can give rise to dislike and suspicion of one's body. I have known several battered wives (emotionally and verbally battered as well as physically) whose husbands or communities have made them feel responsible for their punishment. Their own embodiment generates feelings of disgust and shame. And of course, a well-known manipulative device within many sects and cults is their attempt to control their members through internalized contempt for their own bodily needs.

An even deeper confusion exists about our emotions, which deeply intertwine with our bodily selves. Much spiritual teaching implicitly stresses we are to control our feeling selves rigidly. Many spiritual leaders still teach "self-emptying" as a valid approach to prayer. I continue to hear retreat leaders urging us to leave our worries outside the door. I still hear prayer leaders telling us to breathe in all positive emotions and breathe out all our negative ones.

I am suspicious of this spiritual advice to treat our emotions as naughty children or "chattering monkeys" (as one book put it), shaking them out, breathing them away, emptying them out, or putting them out of the room. I love what Morton Kelsey says about the emptying-out approach to spirituality and meditation:

> Since these feelings do arise essentially within us, it seems on the surface that we should be able to still them to the point of extinction. And once they are under control, why should we let human passions disturb our meditation at all? The idea is very attractive that we should be able to reach a state of perfect relation to the Other that will free us from any disruption in our emotional life.
>
> We forget that the real task is to bring the totality of our psychic being to the Holy, and not just to repress and split off those parts of ourselves that we cannot change. If we deny our emotions, we do one of two things. We may successfully repress them and thus cut ourselves off from one vital source of energy,...or else we dam these emotions up to the point where they break loose on their own..., usually in the most destructive ways.[3]

This awareness of our emotions does not mean that we live at the mercy of every passing distraction and gust of feeling. Rather, it means that when feelings arise, we treat them with respect. They are not marauders but parts of ourselves that we need to look at, listen to, learn from, and then bring to the hands and heart of the Healer.

If we want to focus on something other than a disturbing feeling at the moment it arises, we can respectfully note its inner signal and promise to return later to listen. It is vital then to keep that promise. We never obliterate a feeling; we only drive it down, which increases the underlying problem.

There is another aspect to this attempt to obliterate feelings. Not only do we drive down the problem to the danger point when we silence it, we may also cut off flashing signals of guidance and warning from God. Brennan Manning warns us:

To ignore, repress, or be inattentive to our feelings is to fail to listen to the stirrings and surprises of the Spirit within our emotional structure calling us to the creative response.

Jesus listened. In John's gospel we are told that "he was moved with the deepest emotions" (11:33)....

The gospel portrait of Jesus is that of a man exquisitely attuned to his emotions and uninhibited in their expression. One finds in Christ no attitude of scorn, contempt, fear, ridicule or rejection of feelings....They were sensitive emotional antennae to which he listened carefully and through which he perceived the will of his Father for congruent speech and action.[4]

I began thinking along similar lines some years ago when I read a Lenten booklet in which the writer urged me to renounce all my grumbling during the season of Lent. I found myself thinking rebelliously (holy rebellion!) that this approach to spirituality was not an incarnational one. This approach completely ignored or disregarded the complexities of the human personality. Spiritual teachings have ignored the frontiers of psychotherapeutic discoveries for far too long. This neglect is dangerous, absurd, and unspiritual!

What would happen, I thought, *if instead of giving up my grumbling this Lent, I listened to it for the first time in my life? Listened with respect!* Usually when a negative feeling confronted me, either I tried to drive it down or I just submitted to it. Neither of these approaches is respectful. I might not *do* what my negative feelings direct, but I could try with honesty to listen to what lay at the roots of this grumbling.

I tried listening, and I learned things about myself that I should have learned years earlier. I learned about the victimhood stance. I began to learn about appropriate boundaries and limits. I began to learn about inner refreshment and nurture. I began to learn about most of the things this book stresses.

One particular scripture story became for me a wonderful metaphor of sincere and respectful depth listening: the story of the blind beggar Bartimaeus (Mark 10:46-52) who sits by the roadside hopefully calling out to Jesus to pay attention to him and heal him. Some of the people in the crowd try to hush him up. (Probably they felt, as we so often do, that he should set his mind on "higher things.") The more they try to silence him, the louder he shouts. Jesus turns to him instantly and asks, "What do you want me to do for you?"

Within each of us is that which cries out, begging to be heard. Often the manner of its crying out is expressed through grumbling, negativity, irritability, anxiety. To shout down the cry, to put it out of the room, to breathe it away, or to shake it off is not the Christian, the incarnational way. Let us learn to pay attention, to listen, and to question that which cries out in us: Who are you? What are you trying to tell me? And then let us learn to listen and respond to Jesus' question: "What do you want me to do for you?" It is both astonishing and revealing what will surface if we keep patiently asking and listening to our inner Bartimaeus!

In the previous chapter I spoke of learning to listen to my resistances. It can become a major spiritual discipline to listen, in Christ's presence, to all that appears to be negative thinking. After listening, I bring these feelings and their underlying problems to the Healer. Then I try to discern guidance about appropriate changes in my daily living. Only then do I begin to move off dead center.

One of the most exciting, rewarding spiritual movements of this generation is based upon the research of Dr. Eugene Gendlin of the University of Chicago. He calls his process of self-listening and depth awareness Focusing, and many Christian spiritual leaders and institutes have sponsored it enthusiastically. This approach emphasizes not merely the thinking but also the bodily-emotional feeling about our issues, thus enabling us to listen and respond to our inner Bartimaeus. Authors Campbell and McMahon, referring to Gendlin's description of Focusing, offer these helpful reflections:

Rarely, though, have we been taught *how to be in the hurt*, allowing it to say something about life and ourselves, letting it tell its own unique story....

Deep down, though, our bodies know that this unprocessed experiencing is still there....What makes Focusing unusual is that it creates an inner climate around our painful and frightening issues....Focusing invites us to relate in a different way to what we perceive as unloveable in ourselves....

From a therapeutic point of view, Eugene Gendlin's unique contribution has been to show that surface emotions,...are directly tied to a more rudimentary *felt sense* of how a particular issue is carried in the body....

As Gendlin points out, to feel "unaccountably uncomfortable" means you are aware of more in your body than you can think in your mind.[5]

Gendlin describes six movements of this unfolding process: clearing a space, the felt sense, finding a handle, resonating, asking, receiving. Gendlin's process is one of the most wholesome and fruitful of new Christian spiritual and healing frontiers because of its complete resonance with the scriptural vision of the human being.

The phrase I use, *incarnational spirituality*, came to me with inner spontaneity about fifteen years ago. I had never read or heard the phrase before, though with that strange communal synchronicity that often occurs, I have come across it frequently in recent years. To me, this phrase refers to that relationship with God that encounters, honors, and embraces the full human condition. Incarnational spirituality invites all aspects of ourselves to the Healer who will hear them, who will heal them if they need healing, transform them if they need transformation, affirm and empower them if they need nurture.

When I think of the fullness and inclusiveness of the way God deals with our complex selves—our energies, strengths, gifts, weaknesses—I remember the powerful passage from

Ezekiel 34. In this passage God speaks through the prophet and witnesses to God's care for the sheep in all their varying needs and powers:

> For these are the words of the Lord God:
> "Now I myself will ask after my sheep and go in search of
>   them....
> and rescue them, no matter where they were scattered
> in dark and cloudy days....
> There will they rest, there in good pasture,...
> I myself will tend my flock,
> I myself pen them in their fold,...
> I will search for the lost,
> recover the straggler,
> bandage the hurt,
> strengthen the sick,
> leave the healthy and strong to play,
> and give them their proper food" (Ezek. 34:11-16, NEB).

While the different Bible translations offer various renderings of the final verse, I personally delight in the New English Bible translation, which encourages our healthy, strong members (or inner characteristics) to play! Playfulness is a most neglected aspect of our Christian spiritualities, particularly for the strong ones among us!

REFLECTION AND MEDITATION

(Move very slowly through this meditation.)

> And the Word became flesh and lived among us (John 1:14).

> They will not hurt or destroy on all my holy mountain; for the earth will be full of the knowledge of the Lord as the waters cover the sea (Isa. 11:9).

Rest your body, breathe God's breath of life slowly and gently. Think of God's enfolding love, shown so fully through Jesus.

When you feel ready, ask yourself how you feel about your own "holy mountain"—your human self, bodily and emotional. Do not condemn or preach to your feeling; just note what it is. Rest in the presence of the Incarnate One who knows what you feel.

Let your attention begin to move gently through your bodily self. Notice (without trying to change it) where your muscles feel tight or defensive. You may want to touch that bodily area gently.

Notice where your body feels most vulnerable, powerless. Can you gently touch that place? Do you dislike certain bodily areas? Think of each as touched by God's hand.

Is there special discomfort or pain? Is there a bodily part that has been under great stress recently, which has been working hard for you: eyes, hands, legs, feet, back, etc.? Touch that area gently or think of it with thanks.

Listen to what your body is telling you through these stressed, tight, hurt, vulnerable, disliked areas. What are they trying to tell you about what is happening in your life?

Ask your body what it needs—what *you* need, deep down. Listen, observe quietly the inner feelings, words, pictures, memories, or longings that arise. Take all the time you need.

When ready, think of parts of your body that reflect well-being, strength, joy, vitality. Can you touch one such bodily part? What aspect of your life does this part represent or reflect? What does this strong, joyous bodily part tell you? What can it share with the whole body?

Does some special feeling, need, memory, or problem rise in your heart at this moment? Think of it, or picture it lifted in the arms of the Incarnate One, as you would lift a child.

Now let the light of Jesus Christ unfold like a flower in your heart center, or let it begin to flow like a river of light through your whole body, into the tight muscles, warming and relaxing them; flowing into the vulnerable parts that feel unprotected, forming a protective warmth around them; flowing into the bodily parts you dislike, healing their shame with love; into the overworked, stressed areas with refreshment and renewal. Picture or think of this light flowing with power into every cell of painful or diseased bodily areas.

Now let your whole body feel enveloped in Christ's own cloak of healing. Rest, and breathe in this healing light. As you rest, quietly breathing, reflect on the powerful, mysterious saying: "We are not human beings trying to be spiritual; we are spiritual beings trying to be human!"

Verbal Prayer: If visualization is difficult or uncomfortable for you, simply touch or think of some of these bodily areas listed above, and pray inwardly or aloud: "In the Name, by the Word, and through the Light of Jesus Christ, you are known, heard, loved, enfolded, and renewed" (or other words that may come to you). Say the same prayer for a hurting feeling.

5

Depth Healing: The Leader's Urgent Need

He showed them his hands and his side (John 20:20).

HY DID JESUS STILL HAVE WOUNDS on his risen body? The traditional answer is that the wounds proved it was really he and not an impostor. Carrying and revealing the wounds were acts of swift, discerning mercy for his friends who were in a condition of mixed confusion and suspicion. But I believe the wounds had a deeper meaning with radically transforming implications that affect us through the ages. I believe the wounds were the sure sign that the eternal God through Jesus has never and will never ignore, negate, minimize, or transcend the significance of human woundedness. The risen Jesus is not so swallowed up in glory that he is beyond our reach, beyond our cries. He is among us, carrying wounds, even in a body of light. His every word and act shining forth the meaning and heart of God means that God's heart carries our wounds. God suffers with us.

Is this vision of God's union with our pain the supreme significant vision that is unique to Christianity? Many ancient religions had stories and myths about divine beings who incarnated temporarily as humans or animals. Some of them acted with scandalous selfishness; others brought comfort and healing. But I can only think of two who suffered for and with humanity. Significantly, neither was thought to represent ultimate reality. Each acted on his own, unsupported by the highest gods or forces of the universe.

Some interpretations—both past and present—of Jesus' atonement have seemed to put the nature of Jesus and the nature of God the Creator at variance. The well-known biblical theologian William Barclay wryly quotes in his autobiography a hymn that was much sung in his youth:

> Jehovah lifted up his rod;
>> O Christ, it fell on thee!
> Thou wast sore stricken of thy God;
>> There's not one stroke for me....
> Jehovah bade his sword awake;
>> O Christ, it woke 'gainst thee!
> Thy blood the flaming blade must slake,
>> Thy heart its sheath must be....
>> Now sleeps that sword for me.

Barclay reflects about this hymn and its theology:

> It seemed to oppose God and Jesus, and to present me with a God who was out to punish me and a Jesus who was out to save me....Slowly it began to dawn on me that apart from the love of God there would have been no Atonement at all....Jesus came, not to change God's attitude...but to demonstrate God's attitude...to show what God is like.[1]

The Korean theologian Andrew Sung Park, using the word *han*, which is the Korean expression for the woundedness caused by human hostility and sin, develops the same thought with profound beauty:

> God's love for humans suffers on the cross. The cross represents God's full participation in the suffering of victims....
>
> God's han, the wounded heart of God, is exposed on the cross....
>
> The cry of the wounded heart of God on the cross reverberates throughout the whole of history.[2]

I hope we are emerging from the barbaric theology that would represent God as wrath and Jesus as love, thus separating their nature and slandering the true heart of God. This interpretation was never the teaching of the Gospels. The New Testament makes it very clear that the wounds of Jesus were also the wounds of God, that the love of Jesus was identical with the love of God:

> God so loved the world that he gave his only Son (John 3:16).

> In Christ God was reconciling the world to himself (2 Cor. 5:19).

> [Jesus] is the reflection of God's glory and the exact imprint of God's very being (Heb. 1:3).

But it is not in the crucifixion alone that we see God through Jesus sharing the suffering of the human condition. Jesus bore many human wounds: He was both poor and homeless. He lived in a country occupied by a foreign power. He knew about the temptation of his powers. He knew misunderstanding and rejection by family and friends. He wept when his friend died. He experienced slander, persecution, and the power of political and ecclesiastical injustice. He knew hunger, fatigue, and endless demands and expectations. He never turned from the victims of poverty and disease; he cared passionately about them.

As the "imprint of God's very being," Jesus makes clear to us that God fully enters into and experiences the worst life has to offer, whether in daily life or in the midst of traumatic injustice. We are shown that God passionately cares. Through Jesus' life, we come to know a God who not only shares our wounds and cares about our wounds but a God who longs (which means "wills") for our healing.

Jesus proclaimed the mission of God's spirit within him:

> "To bring good news to the poor,...
> to proclaim release to the captives
>   and recovery of sight to the blind,
>   to let the oppressed go free" (Luke 4:18).

Nothing in this scripture suggests that we take a victim's stance in the face of evil, injustice, disease. All these adversities face us as part of the human condition, but we are not required to submit to them. God's own spirit calls us to release ourselves from our inner prisons and diseases as far as possible. Healing is an enormous part of Jesus' ministry.

But what about the cross? Does not the New Testament tell us to take up our cross as Jesus did? As clearly as I can discern, the New Testament meaning of "cross" implies our free choice to share and remove the burden of pain from another. The cross has nothing to do with illness, accident, or trauma that may come our way. These are more akin to the "thorn in the flesh" (2 Cor. 12:7-8), which God does not send but which God can use. God wastes nothing.

To teach that God deliberately sends us pain is abusive theology. It is like saying that a good parent will throw a child down the stairs to teach the lessons of courage and patience through broken bones! Jesus never told anybody that their pain was God's will for them. Jesus was always on the side of healing and wholeness of every kind.

In his powerful little book *The Will Of God*, the English Methodist pastor and world-known spiritual leader Leslie D. Weatherhead records part of his conversation with a parishioner whose little boy had died horribly of cholera:

> "But John," I said quietly,…"Call your little boy's death the result of mass ignorance, call it mass folly, call it mass sin, if you like, call it bad drains or communal carelessness, but don't call it the will of God." Surely we cannot identify as the will of God something for which a man would be locked up in jail, or put in a criminal lunatic asylum.[3]

Much of the suffering we experience is *not* God's will:

- *the thorn in the flesh:* illness, accident, natural disaster, disability, and trauma of the physical world.

- *the catapult:* sudden traumatic experience of communal, moral evil; sudden emotional rejection and/or injustice; a personal ruptured relationship; the sudden shock of bad news; a traumatic depersonalizing encounter of indifference or hostility.

- *the corrosion:* long-term abuse—physical, verbal, or emotional. Any relationship that has deeply corroded one's sense of self-worth and confidence.
- *the unfulfilled hunger:* chronic deprivation, whether physical or emotional; the pain of lovelessness and lack of warm, emotional intimacy. Within this category I would include long-term loneliness; unhealed grieving; unfulfilled longings and expectations of nations, races, and genders as well as of individuals.
- *the shame:* feelings of innate unworthiness and degradation and humiliation due to one's social, economic, or ethnic position; the wound of being rejected for what one is rather than for what one has done.
- *the depletion:* the chronic exhaustion of overwork, high intensity, draining.
- *the stifling:* the unexpressed inner powers and gifts; the suffering when gifts, talents, and energies are locked up within us due to fear, ignorance, or the repressiveness of those around us.
- *communal toxicity:* the wounding that did not begin with our own personal history but which we have inherited and internalized from a painful family history or from our involvement in a suffering, toxic community. This is one of the most difficult forms of pain to identify and yet one of the most invasive and damaging.

These categories are mine, and of course others may reword and arrange them differently. But as best as I can see, they touch on most aspects of the woundedness of the human condition. I believe that God sends none of these forms of suffering to us as punishment, testing, or for spiritual growth. They come to us as members of the groaning, travailing universe (see Romans 8) as the natural creation works with intertwining human spirit.

They come to us as the shadow side of free will (communal free will more than individual). These wounds and scars need not be wasted, for God can work with and through our wounds and scars. But the Gospels make it clear that God longs to release us from their burden and heal us of their sting.

As mentioned earlier, I put the cross in a separate category from the forms of suffering just listed. The cross always implies our free will and choice to be redemptively involved with someone else's suffering. I do believe that God invites us to the experience of the cross, though it is vitally important that we let ourselves be guided to our *own* real cross.

I also put the suffering related to birthing and transitions in a different category from the forms of suffering *not* sent by God. Growing and changing are painful as well as joyous. I believe God calls us to frequent rebirthing, not because of the pain but in spite of it.

We can distinguish between the cross and the birthing that God *does* send and other forms of pain that God does *not* send by three factors. First, a true cross and a true birthing will include genuine joy along with the genuine suffering. Second, they always involve our free choice; we can choose another way. Third, we experience inherent redemption in these forms of suffering.

The other categories, those of destructive pain, are usually totally joyless. They come to us against our choice and will. There is nothing inherently redemptive about them. By nature they fragment and dehumanize—though God may bring redemption through them if we are willing.

Life within Jesus helps us enter into and embrace the suffering of the true cross and the birth of new beginnings. But life within Jesus also calls us to prevent and heal all those other categories of destructive pain.

It is exciting to see in this past decade far more concern for the healing of both inner and outer wounds than ever before. It excites me to see the growing awareness of the distinction between a sin and a wound, which many of our theologies and spiritualities have so often confused and identified with each other. Also exciting is the increasing number of books and workshops on the healing of the body, the healing of depth wounds of memory, the healing of the whole personality, as well as the healing of communal bodies.

This concern and awareness was not always the case. Even after we all began to grow past the belief that God deliberately sent suffering, still many Christian leaders were apt to take the stance that deliberate staying within suffering implied their solidarity with the pain of the whole world. During my own theological training, it was generally assumed that the more inwardly torn and bleeding you were, the more sensitive and redemptive you would be in ministry. Concern about one's own healing was considered insensitive, noncompassionate, and almost vulgar.

Though not expressed in so many words, the underlying image seemed to be that of Prometheus, benefactor and bringer of fire to suffering humanity, forever chained to his rock with the eagle gnawing at his liver! This image is not that of Jesus who, though still bearing the wounds on hands and side, was most definitely resurrected. It is not enough to say that God is on the cross, sharing our pain—unique and redemptive though that sharing is. God is also the God of resurrection. In fact, the Resurrection not only followed the crucifixion but was inherent in it all along. This inherency is what Jesus explains to the two disciples on the road to Emmaus. (See Luke 24:13-27.) The wounds of Christ are not swallowed up and forgotten; they become radiant centers of deep love and healing. Within the Christian experience, the cross and the Resurrection cannot be divided.

I like very much what James E. Dittes, United Church of Christ minister and Professor of Psychology of Religion at Yale University, says concerning this understanding of pain as solidarity:

> Pain is not the mark of ministry....The minister is not called
> to suffer....The call is *in* the suffering when it happens....
>
> *Calling may be suffered for; suffering is not called for.* (*Italics
> mine.*) The easy misunderstanding that suffering is *called
> for*...leads people to seek the suffering and to suppose that
> simple submission, meek compliance, passive acceptance of
> blows....is sufficient as ministry.[4]

It is fortunate that in recent decades, churches, denominations,
and religious institutions are beginning to take seriously the
emotional well-being of Christian leaders. Some ordination
examining committees are learning ways to discern if a ministerial candidate has chosen ministry to express wholeness or to
find wholeness.

Obviously each of us is a mixed bag of motivations. No one
is totally whole or completely free of unhealed wounds and
unresolved issues. But it is essential that we become aware of our
need for inner healing. Dr. Conrad Weiser, psychologist and an
administrator of systems therapy, shares some grim and startling
observations about wounded healers:

> As many as one-third of professional populations are poten-
> tial abusers or seducers...potential victims or abused...or at
> risk for the potential explosion of severe acting out or for
> the implosion of depression called burnout....
>
> *Systems can no longer assume a certain level of health or
> maturity of candidates for a religious profession....*The damage
> that can be done by immature and dysfunctional religious
> professionals is too great to ignore....
>
> When damaged clergy are linked to damaged systems,
> the results can be catastrophic.[5]

Dr. Weiser makes a strong case for his conclusions that intensive psychotherapy should be a normative part of the preparation for all professional leadership candidates.Whether we agree
or not, clearly our theological schools and our churches need to
give even more serious and informed attention to the unmet

needs and the unhealed inner wounds of all Christian leaders.

It is no secret, for example, that the rapidly increasing divorce rate among clergy is due not so much to weak moral fiber as the fact that clergy families are less willing to endure the obsessive work, the distancing tactics, and even the abusiveness of clergy persons and other religious professionals who are driven frantic by their unhealed wounds and loss of spiritual, emotional renewal. I remember the story told of Carl Gustav Jung. A famous religious leader deeply impressed him. Jung almost decided to become the man's disciple until he met that leader's wife and realized who bore his darkness.

Either clergy sexual abuse is on the rise, or what used to be hidden is now widely publicized. I believe it is inadequate to attribute such abuse solely to ruthless power exploitation. I have met and talked with many of these abusers. Seldom are they cynical, intentional manipulators of power. The ones I have met are desperately confused and hurting, often childish with no awareness of appropriate professional boundaries in their hungry, abortive attempts at intimacy. I am not saying this excuses their actions. The wounds they inflict on the lives and the trust of others is devastating, and their abusiveness must be stopped by whatever means necessary. But the work of the church does not end with stopping the abuser. If the Christian church is truly bonded to the heart of Christ the Healer, then the abuser, no less than the abused, is in desperate need of healing.

For most of us, our inner woundedness does not manifest itself in such extreme ways. Nevertheless, over long periods of time, chronic unhealed pain inflicts subtle but pervasive damage on ourselves and those near us.

Confession is not enough to heal and restore us. This belief that confession alone can heal us and change us at depth has been one of the main errors of the Christian church through the ages. Confession can lift the burden of *sin* and make us clean, but it alone cannot reach the roots of the *wound* and its destructiveness. A sin is an act or choice made in freedom with at least some knowledge of what we do. But when we act destructively or lovelessly out of an inner woundedness, we are not choosing in freedom. We react rather than act. Generally we do not know what we do or why we do it. Therefore, we return to the same problem repeatedly in our confessions, with no real change in result. These repetitive confessions are almost a sure sign that we are dealing with woundedness, which needs healing, as well as sin, which needs forgiveness.

I recall lengthy talks with a woman minister (I have her permission to share this story) who told me she repeatedly fell into the sins of omission. She would neglect the real needs of her friends when she became overloaded with work. She found it hard to forgive herself that she never got around to visiting a personal friend during her last illness. She had intended to but kept putting it off. When the friend died sooner than expected, she could not recover from the shock of what seemed like her loveless neglect. She confided in me that this was a typical pattern of hers. She would always feel remorse, confess this "sinful" behavior, and make good resolutions for the future. But nothing really changed.

As I talked with this clergywoman, I began to realize that remorse, confession, and resolutions would not reach the roots of her problem. She faced the fact that her neglect of those who loved her were not acts done in freedom; thus she could not control her neglect through any "act of will." A deep wound underlay her neglectful behavior.

After some honest reflection, frank talks with those who knew her best, and a lot of praying, this clergy woman began to see a hurtful pattern emerge. She had been brought up by loving parents who were natural leaders and extremely extroverted. Most of her relatives were the same. She had been the submissive, shy follower in the family, assuming that, unlike her parents and siblings, she was not a strong person. When she felt called into ministry, she tried to remake herself into an extrovert. She had no role models for the experience of leadership other than her family members. Ignoring the kind of person she really was, she made no allowances for her basic temperament and plunged into a life without limits and borders. She would go for months wildly overextending herself and then fall into intense lethargy, during which time she could barely carry out her normal responsibilities. Her personal friendships fell through the cracks; she had no time or energy to make friends a priority. To use Jung's concept, the friends carried her darkness.

This story will sound all too familiar to many of us. It certainly did to me. I too know what it is like to flinch at the thought of all the neglected aspects of what was meant to be a life of loving wholeness. For those of us prone to the "sins" of omission, we may neglect our friends or our families or our prayers or our health or active concern for social justice or mental activity or basic housekeeping—or all of these.

Confession alone will neither clarify nor heal such a wounded pattern. Only with a discerning, loving entrance into our secret self and a reconciliation with the person we really are can we begin to understand and remove this burden.

For my friend, prayer enabled the entrance of the living Jesus Christ into the deep place, Jesus the transforming friend who helped her to understand the person she really was and to love that person. She also began to learn she did not have to follow the lifestyles of her family to be a leader and a strong person. She learned there were other ways to be an empowered leader that would allow her to set realistic limits and provide for time alone and replenishing rest. Gradually the years of guilt she had felt at being an introvert with a rather low fatigue level began to fall away from her. She could be who she was, a person loved by God. As the compulsiveness and the attempt to imitate others relaxed their grip on her, she was able to find the time and energy for the people she loved and the things she wanted to do.

Prayer is not necessarily enough to heal us. Some forms of prayer make us worse not better: prayer based on fear of God or fear of one's self, prayer that puts us out of touch with our humanness, prayer that is riddled with guilt and judgment, prayer that pleads and begs God as if God needed flattery and propitiation. Such prayer can deepen our wounds. Such prayer releases within us the harsh inner punisher that we often mistake for God. This harsh punisher is actually the most wounded one of all within ourselves. This inner frightened one loves to play judge; it loves to play God!

But when the true God, who does not condemn but releases, enters our depths with healing power and touches the hurting, frightened, angry children within us, then at last we begin to experience transformation. In reality, of course, that love of God is always within us in those dark, closed places, just as Jesus was in that locked room with his disciples. But now, with our consent, the radical tender healing begins.

My friend's healing took place without the need of therapeutic intervention. After all, she had experienced love from her early family. They overwhelmed but did not abuse. They did not force her to imitate them, though they lacked the sensitivity to discern that she often felt disempowered. But had she experienced emotional or bodily abuse, had she been confined in rigidly limiting categories, had she been made to fear all intimacy, her situation would have differed greatly. She would probably have needed professional therapy along with prayer. We need not feel that, as Christians, we have to choose between professional help *or* prayer. Each enriches and enhances the other. Going to a therapist does not denote lack of trust any more than going to a doctor indicates a lack of trust in God.

Sometimes a wounded person finds the necessary help within a sharing group he or she trusts. When Jesus prepared to heal someone, he often gathered around him two or three trusted friends. They were not giants of faith but ordinary human beings who were present as a consenting community. They were not the source of healing, but I believe their presence helped increase the focused power of the healing. This enhanced, focused power of healing is still available when two, three, or more Christians gather in the presence of the living Jesus Christ.

The church is the community in which this healing is supposed to occur. Tragically, many church liturgies still center around the sin rather than the wound, and they often do not even mention the condition of woundedness. It is also tragic that many churches do not include healing services and healing prayer groups as a matter of course. Churches often fail to emphasize the healing power of the Communion service. I find James Wagner's reflections on this aspect of healing very helpful:

> When we gather at the Lord's table to participate in the sacrament of Holy Communion, we have a unique opportunity to bring our personal insufficiencies to the all-sufficient Christ, to bring our lack of wholeness to receive his complete wholeness....We cannot overstate the health-enhancing possibilities of the sacrament of Holy Communion....The most positive single factor is the total focus on Christ, who is the heartbeat and the source of wholistic, abundant life.[6]

Our involvement with a group of concerned persons, whether inside or outside our church community, can also help us name our wound. I am not speaking of rigid, prescriptive groups that speak out of judgmental and preconceived ideas but a gathering of two or three who can listen without offering instant advice and who can feed back the perceptions they are receiving. I have known several pastors in recent years who have invited a small gathering of informed and trusted friends to sit with them in a process of discernment over a perplexing choice. We can do the same as we attempt to discern wounds and hurts. Encourage such a group to open with prayer, which affirms the real presence of the love of God through Jesus, followed by a short silence within the presence of the Holy One, and then a time of compassionate, focused listening and response.

Not every prayer or sharing group is appropriate for this discernment, however. Morton Kelsey gives us a wise warning:

> Problems and anxieties may arise that are too personal and serious to share with the group. After all, a prayer group is not an encounter group or a therapy group;...I have seen too many people damaged by such encounters where there were no restraints....Encounter groups may have therapeutic value, but *only* when a skilled leader is present to apply the needed checks.[7]

I suggest we ask ourselves the following reflection questions about any healing or listening group or counselor:

- Does this leader or these group members really listen, or do they respond out of preconceived ideas?

- Do they give space for thoughtful silence during and after the listening, or do they instantly give advice and prescription?

- Do they claim to be the only valid source of healing?

- Are my emotions and impressions respected, or does the group or counselor prescribe the emotions I ought to be having?

- Is my timing respected, or am I being hurried into what the group or counselor consider appropriate responses and results?

- Is my free will respected, or am I urged to "surrender" to the group or the leader, even temporarily?

- Am I made to feel guilty about my wound or problem, as if I were personally responsible for the wounding? Is it implied that I have brought it on myself and that I remain caught in my pain because I am personally getting something out of it? (This diagnosis completely ignores the communal aspect—that pain and darkness we may have absorbed from toxic communities around us—of much of our woundedness. I will reflect more on this in a later chapter.)

- Am I told that my suffering is God's will for me as a test or punishment? (Bad theology and worse spiritual therapy!)
- Am I made to feel guilty or ashamed if my healing is delayed or incomplete?
- Am I encouraged to seek professional help, or am I accused of a lack of faith?

In short, we can ask ourselves if our sense of burden, our lack of freedom, and our increased pain are a result of the book, leader, group, or system. If so, then something is wrong, no matter how respected or spiritual the leader or group may be.

As leaders we often find ourselves in the role of listener to someone working through woundedness. Listeners—whether individuals or part of a group—also have responsibilities, questions to ask themselves, and rights. We need to discern some of these aspects:

- Am I able to listen quietly without quick simplistic answers, diagnosis, and advice?
- Am I able to discern and assist in the decision as to whether this problem or wounding is beyond my skills and requires therapeutic professional attention? (This perception is often difficult to admit. It takes a lot of humility to realize that we may *not* be the person sent by God to help the other.)
- Am I able to affirm and encourage the other in self-worth, dignity, and essential empowerment? (It is so tempting to revel in the other person's need of us, but essentially that person needs to feel his or her own freedom and power as soon as possible.)
- Can I encourage the other to trust his or her own instincts and to allow the other to express and define the feelings present?
- Am I able to discern and clarify practical helps? For example, if a person is in an abusive situation, what resources can

I suggest: hotlines, shelters, financial aid centers, and therapeutic or legal references? There is no point in praying about an abusive situation unless we have done all we can to help stop the abuse. Do I know of helpful books, workshops, and resource material for *other* types of wounding?

- Am I able to keep from pushing or rushing the other to conclusions, healing, and closure? Do I have a strong inner agenda for this person?

- Am I aware of my own inner self so that I am not drained by the other? Am I internalizing the darkness or pain of the other within my own body, my own space? Am I aware of the need of appropriate bodily and emotional boundaries between myself and the other? Christian listening, loving, and burden sharing do not require that we be either drained or invaded. (Chapter 9 will provide deeper reflection on this problem.)

- Am I able to pray for and with this person in a way that does not concentrate solely upon the problem but releases the whole person into Christ's healing hands? No matter how skilled and compassionate we may be as listeners, only God, who works through the deep self of the other, understands the full problem and the way healing may best come.

- When listening to the other, do I remember to surround us both with God's light and loving empowerment?

- Am I able to discern when my role as listener and burden sharer has come to a close? This closure may happen naturally and spontaneously as the wounded one experiences the deepening healing and inner empowerment. We need to know when to let go, with the offer of *occasional* future talks.

Sometimes the need to end the listening role arises when the other becomes increasingly and unreasonably demanding of our time and strength and is hostile or depressed when we set limits. Sometimes the other will increasingly ask us (not always openly) to take over his or her choices and decisions. This dependency may flatter and tempt us, but it is always a warning sign to a listener and sharer of burdens. A cult relationship can develop easily just between two people!

Our listening role may have ended its usefulness if the other person begins to project hostility, dependence, or emotional attraction (transference) upon us as they work through deep-seated wounds. Most Christian leaders lack the training or qualifications to guide another person through a deeply unsettling traumatic process. I, like most ministers or leaders, have tried several times to do so, but it was a near disaster once or twice and a failure every time. The signs of transference can creep into the relationship so gradually (though sometimes these signs come abruptly and startlingly) that we do not always recognize them for what they are. We think the other is just experiencing a passing mood, or we think we are doing something wrong. But in true transference, with the other projecting upon us the fear and anger he or she experienced as a child, the emotional intensity will get worse, not better. Again, we need to recognize when we are out of our depth.

Sometimes the fact that nothing seems to be happening at all signals the need to end a listening, burden-sharing role. Months go by, maybe years. The other person obviously enjoys the attention, the relationship, and the talking; but we perceive no observable change in the situation or the person's understanding of it. We realize we are right where we began. The relationship becomes one of endless complaining without real perception or (at the other extreme) fascinating intellectual analysis by the other with no real spiritual or emotional change. This "status quo" relationship can become (usually unconsciously) quite manipulative. The listener, burden sharer, then has to decide whether to maintain this commitment of time and energy indefinitely as a friendly contact without real transformational meaning or to end it. This decision requires clear-sightedness about what we choose to do and why.

If we choose to end a listening, burden-sharing role, we

need to handle the closure with love and gentle firmness. Suddenly cutting off a relationship without preparation and closure can do great damage. Probably the best way to end the relationship is to admit frankly to the other person that we are out of our depth and simply do not have the training to work through his or her special problem. We also need to admit our very real human limits of time and strength, while making clear our continued concern and our promise to pray for him or her. We need to provide references of other trained professionals or institutes for possible contact. We can (if this offer feels instinctively appropriate) agree to be in touch occasionally by phone for limited times.

Above all, we need to remember to ask the Christ to keep surrounding the other, ourselves, the whole relationship, and the future with light and guidance. Theologically, we know the love of Christ is always there; but by thus asking, picturing, and affirming, we lay hold of the reality of the omnipresence of Christ's love and internalize it in a way that becomes deeply affective for us.

We still have much to learn about the frontiers of spiritual healing. Though healing of all kinds was a major aspect of Jesus' ministry, we in the church are barely beginning. Individual pain and wounding are already complex enough for us. Our theologies, our spiritualities, and our systems of healing have scarcely looked at the problem of *communal* pain: that vast, barely touched mountain of racial, ethnic, gender, national, world suffering through the ages.

I recall Leslie Weatherhead's saying impatiently in one of his books that he found it totally unhelpful and ineffective to be asked to pray for Europe, Asia, the Americas, Africa, Australia, and all the islands of the sea in one sweeping, intercessory sentence before he was rushed on to something else! Such praying seems lost in a fog of unreality. We have difficulty praying even for specific communal groups: the sick, the homeless, the imprisoned, the unemployed, the addicted. And yet, until we do begin to learn some of the ways by which we can help focus God's radiant light on these communal groups, we have barely begun to fulfill the healing mandate: "Feed my sheep."

Jesus did not say this to burden us. We are not the healers. God (as we have seen through Jesus) hurts for us and embraces our wounds, which go back through time. God's longing and power is to heal our oceans and mountains of pain. We are asked to awaken, to become aware of the cries around us, to learn the ways to let the risen Christ enfold our hearts and carry them with him to the frontiers of healing. There God will do the work; we will consent, pray, and love within that risen life.

REFLECTION AND MEDITATION

> When he saw the crowds, he had compassion for them,
> because they were harassed and helpless, like sheep
> without a shepherd (Matt. 9:36).

> He [Jesus] came down with them and stood on a level
>   place,...
> And all the crowd sought to touch him,
>   for power came forth from him and healed them all
>   (Luke 6:17, 19; RSV).

Rest your body in whatever way is best for you and take a few deep breaths. Then let your breath become light and gentle.

When you feel ready, picture or think of the globe, the body of the earth, held in the hands of Christ, the hands that are wounded—and also filled with light and warmth. Or, if you prefer, picture or think of God's warm light enfolding, wrapping around the earth. Or inwardly say words like these: "Love of God through Jesus, you are enfolding the body of this earth with love."

Sense or picture or just think of that warm, healing light from the wounded hands and heart of God not only enfolding the body of the earth but streaming through it, filling it with healing light.

As you gently, quietly breathe, think of God through Jesus the Christ breathing upon the earth body. Think of the earth body itself beginning to breathe in God's breath, deeply and slowly, like a living being. Remember that God holds the earth and breathes light and life on it, not you. You are watching and consenting and also being breathed upon.

Picture or think of the earth's dark pain flowing into the hands and heart of the Christ who holds the earth. The pain will not destroy the Christ, for the Christ *is* the heart of God. The heart of God can take in and absorb the centuries-old pain, healing and renewing the earth's energies. We watch, quietly breathe, and give thanks.

When you feel ready, bring your attention to your own major area of woundedness. Has trauma struck you in a devastating way? Are you carrying chronic fear, anger, grief? Do you feel deprived of something you deeply need? Have you been abused? Are you spiritually fatigued and drained? Is communal toxicity infecting you emotionally or spiritually? something else?

Notice your body's responses at this point. Does the main wounding seem focused in a bodily area—eyes, abdomen, face, jaw, hands, back, breathing?

At this point do not try to work through a specific memory of wounding. Just note that the wound exists not only in the past but also somewhere within you: your feelings, your body, your memory.

Picture or sense the risen Christ standing at the center of this painful place, this wound; or sense a warm light forming in this place. You do not have to go there, just watch the light of the Christ shining and expanding with warmth and power there.

At this point of the meditation, you may feel you need to stop for a while. You may sense that the darkness and hurt of that place where the Christ stands begins to be drawn into his heart of light. He is drawing out the toxicity of that wounded place so that when you choose to return there in memory, it will be a healed place. But don't go into specifics now. Just keep your attention and inner eyes focused upon the Christ and the light of the Christ.

If you wish to use inner words at this point, you may say something like this: "Power of love, shining through the risen Jesus, radiantly shine in the dark places of my pain. Let their power to infect me be broken and drawn into your heart."

Perhaps your pain begins to take the form of a little child, a hurt animal, or a broken or drooping plant. Sense or picture how the living Christ lifts it and holds it as long as it wishes.

When you feel ready, picture or think of how the hands that bear the wounds or how the light from God's heart gently touches and enfolds your heart. Rest in the safety of this touch and enfolding. Quietly breathe the reality of God's light. Let your heart rest.

When you feel ready, come slowly forth from your meditation, stretching a little and lightly rubbing face and hands. Give yourself some quiet moments before reentering your usual interaction with others.

6

Walking with Christ to Deep, Wounded Memories

Jesus himself came near and went with them (Luke 24:15).

$\mathcal{T}$ HOSE TWO DISCIPLES ON THEIR WAY to Emmaus that early evening are working through deep levels of shock, grief, disappointment. Memories that burn, disillusion, and bewilder are very much with them. Then the stranger joins them, walks with them, enters their sad conversation, and begins to unfold for them the meaning of what has happened. Though they do not recognize him until they all sit together at supper, even on that healing walk their hearts burn within them as he talks with them (Luke 24:32). I am sure this warming of their hearts comes not just from his words but also from his presence with them.

What God says to each of us in the healing of our pain differs widely, for each person's wounds are unique. But the healing presence is the same for us all. Christ's presence is the source of healing power that sets our hearts on fire, a very different fire from the burning of unhealed memories.

For many of us, the walk to Emmaus has become a radiant scriptural metaphor for our transitional times, for our unfolding and growing in the life of Christ. This Bible story holds so many meanings. For me, the walk to Emmaus also reflects our walk with the risen Christ to whatever has hurt us and still has a strangling, infecting hold on us.

"But why go back?" I sometimes hear. "Surely we should put our hurts behind us, forgive and forget (as good Christians should), and go on with our lives." But our attempts to heal a memory smoldering in our deep selves with commands to forget and forgive will not heal us any more than mere confession can heal a wound. A memory can keep burning within our inner selves for years or keep replaying in our thoughts like recorded music on a repeat track. Sometimes the memory replays itself on the conscious level, sometimes within the subconscious.

As an example of the conscious replaying, once a close friend became furious with me when I could not automatically include her in some long-range plans I had made. Her hurt and rage were traumatic to both of us. Though I had to stick to my decision, the emotional shock took a long time to heal. For months, quite compulsively several times a day, I rehearsed and replayed those upsetting scenes: what she said; what I said; why all this had happened in the first place. The lack of an intentional act of healing between us made the situation worse because there was no closure to the incident, neither then nor later. I felt as if part of me had gotten stuck at that point in time. I was reminded of those ghost stories in which the ghost keeps returning to the scene of the crime for centuries—often dragging chains! I certainly felt as if part of me were chained to that incident.

As an example of subconscious replaying, I had a shock one night while alone at the church I was serving as a student pastor. A homeless man had come into the church and had hidden in a closet to sleep. I opened the closet door to put something away, and we both scared each other almost witless! No harm was done. He ran away at once and never returned. I scolded myself for not locking the doors when I was alone there at night. I told others about the event and finally laughed and shrugged it off. I seldom gave it another thought. I had no idea of the real depth of the shock until I returned to the same church the following summer and discovered I was unable to walk into the building alone, even in the daytime! I felt total panic with all the classic symptoms of delayed shock: pounding heart, sweats, chills, feelings that the walls were closing in! Fortunately this time a dog came as a package deal with the parsonage. Every time I went near the church, I took the dog with me. Having him with me was the only way I could control my panic.

In those days I knew nothing about the healing of memories. But those two incidents began to take on significance as I learned more about the whole process of inner healing. They were small wounds compared to what many other people have gone through, but they clearly demonstrated to me the fact that part of one's self can get locked into the past. The rest of one's self may move on, but the wounded part remains trapped. Not only is it trapped, but sometimes it smolders or corrodes. Either way, it certainly affects our present life and relationships in both subtle and overt ways. We all know what happens when some minor incident or association wakens a deep hurtful memory: We usually overreact and unload anger or fear from long ago on the innocent bystander of today. Somewhere I read or heard of a woman's saying that her deep wound acted like a magnet. Ever after, anything that reminded her of her wound flew straight to that sore spot like pieces of metal, and all her reactions were overreactions.

These past wounds go beyond trapping us at a point in time. Apparently actual physiological changes take place in the brain. The Linns tell us:

> Not only do our behavior patterns reveal past hurts, but even physiological studies of the brain show that everything that has happened to us remains a part of us. In 1951 Dr. Wilder Penfield, a neurosurgeon at McGill University, found that if he stimulated a certain area of the brain during surgery, the patient would recall a certain past incident as if it were being reenacted with all the feelings experienced when the incident originally took place....We carry not just past memories, but the pain or love associated with those memories.[1]

The authors (who do some of the most helpful memory healing in this generation) continue with this explanation:

> We can get untrapped from the negative effects of past
> hurts and turn those hurts into gifts for loving by bringing
> Jesus' love into hurtful memories....We are not asking him
> to erase or help us forget the past. Rather, we are asking
> Jesus to "heal our memories."[2]

The authors are careful to emphasize that we cannot rush or
push the process of healing. They also tell us not to push the
process of forgiveness if another person has wounded us. We
need to face anger, to accept it as part of the healing Christ
brings. Jesus never repressed anger at injustice or abuse.

Some time ago, it occurred to me that two kinds of anger
exist. Clean anger, which occurs when we know why we are
angry and at whom or what we are directing our anger, is
cleansing and therapeutic—and scriptural. Infected anger is the
murky, all-pervasive smoldering kind, whose roots and origin
are unclear. This anger eats from within and/or lashes out at the
innocent when associations provoke it. There is a difference
between a person who is angry and an angry person.

However, even clean anger can become infected and
destructive if it finds no expression or means to change the situation. Any time we submit to an abusive or hurtful situation
(even when others have not intended harm) out of fear or not
wishing to "make waves" or because we think resistance is not
Christian and we try to swallow our anger, we do devastating
harm. We harm not only ourselves but eventually those around
us. The repressed anger will begin to make itself felt in countless little negative ways.

When we push and rush the process of forgiveness in a
simplistic way, we often deepen the problem of murky, infected anger. In any process of forgiveness we need to take the
time to move through these stages, though not necessarily in
this order:

- We need to be able to name the hurt, abuse, injustice, or
  trauma.

- We need to take steps to feel safe by setting firm limits, emotional distancing, or leaving the situation if necessary.

- We need (very soon) to get in touch with our own inner empowerment and our freedom. We often overlook this step, but it is essential. The sense of powerlessness is one of the most destructive results of woundedness and usually opens the door for more abuse or hurt.

- We need to rebuild our sense of self-esteem and self-value. Often (paradoxically) we feel deep shame at our own selves after having been hurt or abused.

- We need to take time to work through grief and anger, especially by sharing what we feel with others we trust.

- We need to be intentional about undertaking some form of memory healing. We need to make sure that the method we use or the guide we may choose to lead us does not push us but gives us permission to stop the process at any point.

- In time (perhaps much later) we can begin to see the other as victim also. Hurts are passed from person to person and from generation to generation. When this realization starts to unfold, we often can begin to pray for the other's healing.

- Along with this step, we can begin to release the other from our expectations. No one can "make up" for past harm, so we eventually will need to free him or her and ourselves from the prison of resentment. This freedom from resentment does not mean that we are willing to go back to the old destructive ways of relating. Whether we can establish a new relationship with the other or not, we must tell the truth and maintain integrity.

- Finally, during and after the healing of any hurt in the forgiveness process, we need to ask ourselves what we have learned from the experience. What have we learned about ourselves and other people? What have we learned about God? God does not send hurt, but no hurt need be wasted.

In the meditation that follows, I have suggested either a visualizing process or an inwardly spoken process for those who are uncomfortable with inner picturing. I also give suggestions for bodily response. This meditation is not only for the healing of a relationship wound; you may use it for any trauma of hurt, fear, or grief, such as an accident, illness, or bad news.

If at any point you feel frightened or in extreme pain, withdraw from the meditation at once and move into some other form of prayer. Or just stop praying for the time being. Your not continuing to pray does not mean that you have left God's presence or that you lack faith. It may mean that you can work through this particular memory best with a trained counselor or with an experienced group or that you need more time to feel safe and empowered before working through this memory.

You may find you need time to talk about the experience and your feelings before you undertake a healing meditation, especially if the wound is recent or if a memory of a hurt has just surfaced with all its significance. Often we need a distancing and a feeling of safety before we can begin to pray about particularly hurtful memories.

But we need to remember that God is in every step of this process of healing and forgiving, not just when the praying begins. Whether we can pray right away about our pain or not, we have not left God's presence for a minute nor has God left our presence for a minute. Through Jesus, we have seen how God stands with us in our pain, just as Jesus stood in that locked room with his wounded, grieving, frightened, angry, exhausted disciples that glowing Easter night.

As we have seen through Jesus that night, God does not pressure or rebuke us. Through Jesus, God shows God's own wounds and vulnerability—this God who has forever renounced force over us.

And in that sharing by God and in the trusting touch of the disciples, the Resurrection relationship began. It begins for us in the same way.

REFLECTION AND MEDITATION

"When I go and prepare a place for you,
I will come again and will take you to myself,
that where I am you may be also" (John 14:3, RSV).

Relax your body in whatever way is most comfortable. Take a
few deep, slow breaths, then let your breathing become quiet
and gentle. Know that the Healer is close. How does the Healer
seem to come to you today? as the image or thought of Jesus as
he healed and blessed? as a sense of warmth, light, cradling arms,
or hands? Trust what seems to come.

When you feel ready, ask God's spirit to guide you to a
memory of some hurtful experience. You may not be ready at
this time inwardly to walk back through this experience yourself; even if you are, ask Christ the Healer to go back into that
time and place *ahead* of you. The place of the experience itself
needs healing. As if you were watching from afar, picture or
think of the Healer's going to that location, whether a room, a
house, a workplace, an office, a hospital, or some outdoor place.
Picture or think of the Healer standing in the center of that
place of pain, just as he stood behind the locked doors where
the disciples huddled in fear. Picture the Healer holding out his
own wounded hands and absorbing the pain, darkness, and toxicity of the place through his own hands. God takes the threatening associations directly into God's own heart, where that
dark energy will be cleansed and renewed into the energy of
light.

Picture how the light shines from the Healer's heart and fills
that place to the full with light till it saturates the floor, walls,
entrances. Let the peaceful light radiate from the whole cleansed
place.

This may be all you wish to do at this time. If so, end the
meditation here with full but gentle breathing. You may come
back later.

But if you choose to proceed, you may ask the Healer to

come back for you and walk with you to that cleansed place. If ready, enter the space, and feel its safety. Just rest there for a while, breathe in the light and the freshness of the new life. Again, this much of the meditation may be enough for you at this time: to experience the safety of the place with the Healer. If so, walk back to this present time.

But if ready, ask the Healer to invite another person involved in the hurtful memory into the space with you. (If the memory involved several persons, you may wish to have a separate healing prayer for each of them.) Let the other enter in whatever way feels best for you. Some wish to see the other as a child—the hurt and hurtful child within that person. That often seems less threatening, especially if the other person involved in your hurt was a person in authority over you. But if you prefer to picture the other as you remember him or her, that is all right too. If you feel threatened, ask the Healer to stand *between* you and the other or to hold you while the other is in the room.

Remember you are in a safe place. The full protective power of the Healer is with you, enfolding you. Nothing can harm you.

Let yourself feel what you do feel and express what you need to express, whether anger, grief, disappointment, outrage, desolation. Whatever you feel will not shock your Healer. God has known already what you felt. You do not need to speak or even look at the other person involved at this time if you do not wish to.

This may be all you choose to work through at this time. If so, walk back to the present time with the Healer. But if you feel ready, picture the Healer's inviting the other person to share some feelings. Keep remembering that you are in a safe place and that nothing can harm you.

After a while (maybe after several memory sessions) you may wish to speak with the other person in the presence of the Healer. You may wish to hear more of that person's wounds, grief, fear. Eventually you may be ready to exchange a gift or some other sign of reconciliation. But do not rush this process.

If the wounded memory involves an accident, sudden ill-ness, a traumatic moment of unexpected bad news, or a natural disaster, again picture the Healer's going ahead of you to that time in the past to transform the toxicity of associations and to put arms of protection and blessing around the whole place. Sense the infinite love flood through the location. When you feel ready, go with the Healer back to that point in time. Stand in that place and feel the infinite safety, the endless ocean of light holding you. Nothing can harm the you who are the eternal child of God.

> "My sheep hear my voice. I know them....
> I give them eternal life, and they will never perish.
> No one will snatch them out of my hand"(John 10:27-28).

When ready to leave your meditation, picture the radiant light so filling that place of memory that even when you are not consciously there, the cleansing and transformation will continue. Let the light of the place of memory shine along your path as you return with the Healer to this present time, blessing and healing this present moment.

Rest quietly in this present time and place, giving thanks. When ready, become slowly aware of your bodily self, the room around you. Stretch a bit and conclude your meditation gently.

Verbal and bodily prayer for healing a specific memory

If picturing and visualization are uncomfortable for you, other approaches can be just as effective. You may wish to try them even if you are a visualizer.

Relax your body; breathe gently, deeply, and slowly; then forget about your breathing. Let it flow naturally. Sit quietly for a few minutes, thinking about the love of God, perhaps reading a favorite hymn, or inwardly repeating a verse about God's love such as John 10:27-28 quoted above.

When ready, notice if any place in your body feels tense, stressed, defensive, or vulnerable. Lay a gentle hand (if you can do so comfortably) upon that bodily part. Does this bodily tension seem associated with any special unhealed memory?

You may either keep your hand on that special body area or both hands on your heart area. Or, if you prefer, hold in your hand some memento of the hurtful experience: a photo, a letter, a garment, or any other symbolic object that you associate with the wound.

You may choose to close your eyes. You may prefer to look at a picture of Jesus or a cross. Or you may wish to experience God's healing through nature by looking at a flowering bush, a strong tree, a mountain, water, or the blue sky.

Then say aloud or inwardly, "Holy Spirit of Jesus Christ, Healer and Comforter, enter this place of pain within me .... Touch this place of pain....Breathe on this place of pain ....Heal this place of pain....Fill it with your radiant light...."

Pray this prayer slowly with long pauses. Repeat it as often as you wish.

After some moments of quietness, say, "I give you thanks." Breathe slowly and deeply four or five times, and gently end your prayer time when you wish.

If you choose, lay your memento in the sun or under a cross or even put it in the ground under a flower bush. This ritual of closure may help you if you feel comfortable doing it. Some other symbolic bodily gesture may occur to you that will serve as a sign to your whole self that this memory will no longer be a source of toxicity for you but a new beginning, a new strength, a new compassion.

7

Spiritual
Exhaustion
and
Depth Renewal

*Jesus…took the bread and gave it to them
(John 21:13).*

THEY WERE NOT JUST TRAUMATIZED and wounded men; they were exhausted men. Anyone who has suffered shock and grief knows how deep and pervasive the fatigue is. After the first adrenaline response to emergency, tiredness spreads swiftly throughout the body and mind. Emotional responses begin to shut down. One wishes to sleep forever, but sleep is short and broken. Oddly enough, great unexpected joy with its radical change in one's life is also high on the stress list, eventually bringing deep temporary fatigue.

Jesus' disciples had experienced the shock of the betrayal and the inexpressible grief, which came on the very heels of Palm Sunday's triumph. Then they had experienced the hostility of the community, their own danger, the empty tomb, the flying rumors of the Resurrection, and finally the shock of joy on Easter night.

Even after the Resurrection, we still sense the disciples' bewilderment and uncertainty. Why does John's Gospel tell us of their sudden decision to go fishing? Is it an instinctive longing to get back to the old, accustomed ways? Do they want some distance from those overwhelming perplexities of shock, grief, joy, and bewilderment all combined? We can imagine their thoughts: *What will come next? Better not to ask. Anything can happen now. At least fishing is a sure thing.* They understand about fishing. That is what they had done before they met Jesus.

But even the fishing lets them down. They fish all night with no results. No fish, no sleep!

Then in the early morning freshness they see him. He stands on the beach by the water's edge and calls out to them. He tells them where to let down the nets for a haul, then invites them to the shore where a fire and a cooked breakfast await them. He breaks the bread and the cooked fish and serves them. Only then does he start the deep healing of Peter's shame and grief and give him the mandate to reach out to all the hungry sheep of the world. First, Jesus ministers to his disciples' tiredness.

For most of us in Christian leadership, the pervasive tiredness is not usually the result of a series of climactic crises. For most of us, it accumulates so gradually over months and years that we do not recognize it. Spiritual exhaustion and/or chronic inner tiredness does not always manifest itself in outer tiredness. Its symptoms are widely diverse. Spiritual exhaustion may manifest itself as restlessness; compulsive overworking; irritability; numbing of emotional response; mood swings; compulsive and escapist eating, drinking, reading, exercise, television watching. It can cause heavy prolonged sleep or restless broken sleep. We may experience unusual amounts of daydreaming, difficulty in concentration, intense longings for solitude or an equally intense need to be with others. Feelings of hopelessness and powerlessness often accompany spiritual exhaustion. Eventually the body's immunity weakens. I have noticed that when I begin to feel inappropriately anxious or nervous, it is for me anyway an unfailing sign of deep inner tiredness.

Obviously these symptoms can have other causes, so we need to have them medically checked out. It is especially important to rule out the beginnings of clinical depression. But even if we discover that illness or depression is the problem (perhaps I should have said *especially* if illness or depression is the problem), we need to ask if something in our life is causing this exhaustion.

Monica Baldwin's autobiographical account will sound familiar to many Christian leaders:

As a rule, one is first attracted to prayer by the joy and sweetness one finds in it....

And then—often suddenly and for no apparent reason—the sunshine vanishes. Instead of the warmth and colour that have hitherto permeated everything, a dreadful depressing greyness...blights every detail of one's life like a bleak east wind....The entire spiritual world seems meaningless and unreal; even one's own most vivid spiritual experiences fade out like half-forgotten dreams. One becomes keenly, sometimes agonizingly aware of everything prosaic....

Worse, one's condition is often aggravated by odd, inexplicable stupidities of hand and mind. One drops, spills, breaks, upsets and loses things: forgets one's duties, does one's work badly and finds oneself in awkward situations that lead to humiliation and reproof. Bitterest of all, one is beset by horrible temptations to see in Religious Life the most fantastic of all delusions and oneself as a pathetic fool for having undertaken it.

Normally one would turn to prayer as an escape from all these tribulations. But to those in the grip of real spiritual desolation, the hours of prayer are perhaps the hardest of the whole depressing day.[1]

Baldwin calls this experience spiritual desolation, and certainly it is. But my guess is that most of the underlying cause is severe inner fatigue and spiritual exhaustion.

Reports of just what percentage of Christian leaders are experiencing severe fatigue vary widely. Depending on the survey, it varies from thirty percent to seventy-five percent. But all reports agree that the percentage is astonishingly high for a profession in which the work schedule is flexible and is supposedly grounded in depth relationship with the Source of all energy, love, and strength!

When unhealed fatigue reaches a certain point, we begin to avoid the very things that offer us the hope of refreshment and renewal. The very condition of *being* renewed seems too demanding. I recall a time of my own illness and fatigue when the brilliant red of a Christmas poinsettia was too stimulating in its vibrancy. Even looking at it made me tired, and I finally asked my husband to take it from the room and put it where I would not have to see it.

In the same way, I have sometimes avoided the very prayer time that I knew would help me. I have sometimes avoided reading a challenging book or pursuing a helpful personal encounter *because* I know it will give me the strength I need. At the moment, I don't want that strength. I want to be left alone to rest, even from God. Such contrary behavior is similar to our avoidance of exercise even when we know we are tired because our circulation is poor. A brisk walk would make all the difference, but because we are so tired we don't want the difference. Thus a vicious cycle begins. The more tired we are, the less we want to put out a hand to take the very things that will help us.

As I reflect on this strange paradox, I think I understand at least one of the possible meanings of that mysterious comment in John 21 as the disciples head their boat toward land in response to Jesus' invitation: "Now none of the disciples dared to ask him 'Who are you?' because they knew it was the Lord" (vs. 12).

Yes, I understand that. Often I have not asked, "Who are you?" to a challenge from God just *because* I know who it is. If I ask, I will get an answer—and then I will have to do something about it. Even worse, God will supply the energy to do something about it! And right now, that is the last thing I want!

In my earlier ministry, I simply accused myself of laziness at such times. A pejorative categorization explained my condition and neatly pigeonholed it. Slowly I learned to ask the deeper questions of inner resistances and other "negative" responses: "Who are you? What are you telling me? Are you coming from some deep fatigue in my life?"

Slowly I have learned (and so often forget), when another Christian leader comes to me to share the problem of spiritual fatigue and lethargy, *not* to say, "Oh, what you need is more daily prayer discipline, more exercise, more involvement with others—and here is a reading list full of wonderful books that will get you going!" I'm trying to learn to say, "Let's look and listen together for the causes of such spiritual fatigue in your life."

The causes of such inner fatigue are legion and complex. You may wish to reflect on the following questions:

Do I believe that a minister or Christian leader "ought" to be willing to be worn out for others? We looked at this problem in the previous chapters on woundedness, and we will reflect upon it again in the chapter on spiritual draining. This concept—that the more one is exhausted in the service of others, the more worthy one is in the sight of God, oneself, and others—is one of the most deep-seated and hard-to-heal causes of inner fatigue.

Do I have unrealistic self-expectations? This relates closely to the problem just stated, of course. We feel as if we should be the source and never-ending fountain of love, redemption, good cheer, and fortitude at all times and in all places. We have inner images of everything's going to pieces if we do not hold it all together. We use words like *ought* and *should* a great deal about ourselves and feel guilty when we are ill, tired, grieving, bewildered.

Do I find it difficult or humiliating to receive help from others? It was almost impossibly difficult for Peter to let Jesus wash his feet at the Last Supper, although Jesus had let Mary of Bethany wash his feet just the week before (John 12:3). Christian leaders have trouble sharing needs and feelings with others. This problem is often rooted in our perception of our role as primarily servants of others and of God (see chapter 2), rather than as the friends and the beloved who delight in receiving as well as giving.

Do I have few or no borders and boundaries in my leadership? This problem is almost universal. Because we work primarily with other people, our work may not have clear limits and clear closures. The roots are always dangling. I know one pastor so devastated by this problem that he gradually began abandoning all his pastoral responsibilities *except* his perfectly designed liturgical service each Sunday. That task could be finished, completed with no dangling ambiguities, and rewarded with satisfactory feedback. How often we long for a clearly defined eight-hour-a-day job with observable results and definite closures. The lack of clarity and definite limits in our work makes saying no or drawing reasonable limits for ourselves extraordinarily hard. The whole concept of limits becomes murkily ambiguous.

Do I always feel I should be doing more? While closely related to the previous question, this question's roots go deeper than the problem of professional limits. Even in rest times or holidays, many of us feel a need to be nonstop in our self-improvement, our creativity, our spiritual disciplines, our intercessory prayer, our cultivation of the mind, our social justice concerns. "Onward and upward forever!"

This nonstop pace often is tied to a genuine passion for our work and a genuine longing to experience life fully: to go through every open door, to seize every opportunity, to join every good cause, to sign up for all the workshops. We can reach the point where our genuine gifts wear us out because they are so exciting we don't know when to stop!

But for some, the problem finds its roots in a deep dissatisfaction with self. All my life I've heard quoted that ancient but pernicious old saying, "God is easy to please but hard to satisfy." At first this advice sounds wise and accepting, but actually it is extremely damaging both spiritually and emotionally. How would we feel if our spouse said, "Yes, you do often please me, but basically I'm not satisfied with you"? How are children affected if we never give them the feeling that their poems, gifts, school performance, or chores delight *and* satisfy us?

Obviously we need to be honest about a genuine cause for

dissatisfaction. But in a daily, ongoing relationship, chronic dissatisfaction is totally toxic, spreading like poison into families, communities, and whole cultures. Unfortunately, we often consider constant dissatisfaction to be a sign of love and concern for the other, thinking that only through this means can we help ourselves or another keep growing and improving.

Actually, dissatisfaction is the worst possible environment for healthy growth. Without honest praise (too often confused with spoiling or flattery), we become starved of self-esteem and joyous empowerment. When honest praise is withheld, some experience hopelessness, others chronic frustrated anger. The deprivation of honest praise can cause wounds that are felt for a lifetime. This deprivation can cause us to feel we must always be doing more in order to earn full acceptance from others.

I wonder if this desire and need for honest praise is one of the main reasons the scriptures keep urging us to open our mouths and give praise? Joyful praise that expresses delight in God, another, oneself is the essential food for wholeness.

Am I drained by the darkness and toxicity of others around me? This serious source of deep inner fatigue can affect us over generations in our families and is often a cause of exhaustion in daily professional relationships. I reflect on this problem in depth in chapter 9.

Are my prayer life and spiritual disciplines themselves stressful and tiring? Often the very spiritual responses intended for our renewal have become sources of burdensome fatigue. This is especially true if we become rigidly inflexible in our personal prayer discipline, or if we have entered a discipline unsuited to our personality and our unique way of responding. This issue will be considered at length in chapter 10.

Have I increasingly abandoned daily intentional communication with God? As I shared in chapter 1, this neglect was certainly one of the several causes of my own deep fatigue in ministry. I simply had given up the daily deep drinking from the Source of life. For me that grief of God as expressed through Jeremiah had become true:

> They have forsaken me,
>   the fountain of living waters,
>   and hewed out cisterns for themselves,
>   broken cisterns,
>   that can hold no water (Jer. 2:13, RSV).

Even though I have been in a specialized ministry of spiritual renewal for twenty-seven years and even though I have learned the forms of spiritual response that most fulfill my personality type, nevertheless sometimes I forget the intentional drinking each day from the Source. For me, the intentional drinking does not need to be in the same way or at the same time each day or for the same length of time. But if I do not drink at all, deep fatigue is the inevitable result.

Have I been in unrelieved, one-sided intensity recently? Unrelieved intensity over anything eventually causes deep lassitude. Strangely enough, this intensity may include times of prolonged, deep spiritual change and growth. Evelyn Underhill, one of the most gifted spiritual writers and leaders of this century, wrote that the "dark night of the soul," which nearly all the great mystics experienced sooner or later, often is rooted in fatigue:

> Psychologically considered, the dark night is an example of the operation of the law of reaction from stress. It is a period of fatigue and lassitude following a period of sustained mystical activity....However spiritual he may be, the mystic—so long as he is in the body—cannot help using the machinery of his nervous and cerebral system in the source of his adventures....Each great step forward will entail lassitude and exhaustion for that mental machinery which he has pressed into service and probably overworked.[2]

From the *spiritual* perspective of inner fatigue, Underhill has a most interesting insight:

The Dark Night, then, is really a deeply human process, in which the self which thought itself so spiritual, so firmly established upon the supersensual plane, is forced to turn back, to leave the Light, and pick up those qualities which it had left behind. Only thus,...not by a careful and departmental cultivation of that which we like to call [one's] "spiritual" side, can Divine Humanity be formed.[3]

Thus Underhill makes a significant point here: The intensity of the spiritual quest and experience is not the only element that can exhaust us; even more exhausting is the frequent one-sidedness of the intensity. Jesus invites us to "be perfect, therefore, as your heavenly Father is perfect" (Matthew 5:48), but a more accurate translation of the word *perfect* is "whole." Jesus is not enjoining us never to make a mistake or to renounce our humanity. We are called into wholeness, which means to bring all our aspects, all that we are into God's presence, God's light. Building that trust will take time. Entrusting to God those parts of ourselves that we had not thought "spiritual" enough will take time and healing. God loves us in our totality.

What Underhill says about exhaustion's stemming from intensity, especially one-sided intensity, is characteristic of any prolonged, sustained intensity in our ministries: depth counseling, intense study, a long period of sharing the pain of another. During any special demand with its necessary focused power, being intentional about Sabbath interludes is essential.

Am I carrying around within me great burdens of unhealed woundedness? This vast inner load, the focus of chapters 5 and 6, is one of the most toxic, destructive forms of fatigue. It inevitably affects and infects those around us. As mentioned earlier, the healing of wounds that all human beings need is *urgently* needed by the religious leader who has the potential to do so much harm through his or her repressed anger and fear.

Am I constantly expecting my ministry and those involved with it to fit into my categories and agendas? Exasperation and fatigue besets so many strong, gifted leaders (parents and spouses too, for that matter). Changes in plans, interruptions, surprises, unexpected disruptions can cause deep frustration in a highly structured person who has developed clear and concise plans. In the long run this frustration can cause a hopeless, angry tired-ness. Sometimes the leader genuinely is more gifted than the rest of us in envisioning the unfolding of a plan or program. But sometimes the leader's fatigue is rooted in a deep anxiety that cannot tolerate ambiguity or challenging changes. Invariably and inevitably, however, the very nature of ministry must include the unexpected, the surprises, and the interruptions. Undoubtedly one of the most exhausting challenges of ministry is to be simultaneously the efficient, well-organized leader who "runs a tight ship" and the flexible, open-ended leader who tol-erates ambiguity with grace!

The problem of this challenge stretches back to the earliest days of Christianity. Paul, for example, reflected on the neces-sary balance between the spontaneous outbursts of enthusiasm and tongue speaking in worship with the need that "all things should be done decently and in order" (1 Cor. 14:40).

I quoted earlier from James E. Dittes's book *When the People Say No*, which has helped me the most in dealing with the everyday surprises, disruptions, general resistances, and unexpectedness within ministry. I like what he says about our constant temptation to confront the unexpected with rigid agendas:

> The God who refused to be confined to a temple or to a set of laws, to the expectations of disciples or Palm Sunday crowds or crucifying enemies, to the structures of thought or of organization throughout the church's history—that is the God who refuses to be confined to any definition of ministry or agenda for the day, however valid and right that definition may be.
>
> There is, indeed, *an eerie link between agendas and suffering* (*italics mine*). The tighter the agenda, the more painful is any

disruption of it. Disruption does not produce the suffering. Disruption is only disruption; it inflicts pain only if there is a tautness....The tense body is damaged by the blow that the relaxed body rebounds from. It is undue reliance on the law that makes the law, or its breaking, damaging.[4]

Am I entering a time of deep inner shift and growth? Most ministers and other Christian leaders sooner or later experience that deep, disturbing, exciting inner shift that signals something is changing—something new is developing or growing within us. It is rather like a slow earthquake! We may experience a change in dreams or in interests. Deep bodily and emotional energies may awaken. Old ways of living, old hobbies, even former relationships may become unsatisfying. We may feel a sense of restlessness, impatience, energy alternating with fatigue.

Often these inner changes signal new guidance from God. Perhaps we are being invited into a new form of ministry, such as chaplaincy in place of parish work or parish work in place of counseling or counseling in place of administration or the other way around. Perhaps we are being guided not into another form of ministry but into a different way of living our present ministry, with a new rhythm, a new focus, new priorities, new inner spaces. Perhaps we are being called to send down deeper roots into our personal way of spirituality. New gifts may be unfolding, or old forgotten gifts may be awakening. In any case, the call is to freshness and new creativity.

Misunderstanding or resisting this call can lead to profound conflict and inner fatigue. A significant scriptural metaphor for this condition might be seen in Jonah's flight from God's call to Nineveh, the resultant storm at sea, and his attempted escape through his sleep in the ship's hold. We do experience a storm and exhaustion when we resist the call to a new inner life, and often we try to escape through inner anesthetics or addictions. But if we listen carefully to this profound summons (perhaps with the help of friends or spouse in a discernment process), the way will open to the most exciting unfolding in our Christian ministry or leadership that we have ever known.

Occasionally persons involved in deep and rapid spiritual change and growth may have some startling and disconcerting experiences: sudden surges of powerful, tingling energy throughout the whole body or parts of the body or sudden perceptions of inner or outer surrounding light. We may hear sudden sounds like a rushing wind or experience sensations like rising out of the body. We may see or sense other presences in the room. We may experience a new clairvoyant sense of events yet to come or events occurring far away.

Those who are spiritually awakening seem to be experiencing these phenomena in increasing numbers in recent decades, though such experiences are by no means universal. Such phenomena are ancient, well-attested experiences of spiritual awakening, which different cultures and religious traditions call by different names. Probably in such experiences, the neurological system is giving signals of the spiritual energies that are pouring in and moving within us. For most people, the whole process is so slow and gradual that we have few or no sensory signs, although most of us will have an awareness of deeper intuitiveness and more sensitive perception.

Obviously it is good sense to have unusual, disconcerting symptoms checked out medically. But if one's general health is good; if one's daily life is active, responsible, and satisfying; if one's relationships are fulfilling; if no moral degeneration or deep disturbances of inner peace occur, there is no reason to fear mental illness or demonic infestation. It's senseless that so many Christians are both ignorant and fearful of these ancient, widespread spiritual phenomena.

If such phenomena occur, meet with an experienced spiritual director or counselor who can discuss the process and suggest well-balanced, informative books.[5] (See note 5, chapter 7 for two recommended books.) It is also important to eat healthful, nourishing food; to exercise in the fresh air; and to get plenty of rest. Consider temporarily moving away from long, intense meditations into shorter prayers throughout the day.

Scripture indicates many such experiences, though most of the scriptural examples unfold into a full mystical vision, a clear voice of God, or outstanding gifts of the Spirit. In the Hebrew Scriptures, for example, the prophet Ezekiel tells us:

> Then the spirit lifted me up, and as the glory of the Lord rose from its place, I heard behind me the sound of loud rumbling (Ezek. 3:12).

Or from Job:

> Now a word came stealing to me,
>   my ear received the whisper of it.
> . . . .
> A spirit glided past my face....
> It stood still,
>   but I could not discern its appearance (Job 4:12, 15-16).

We may think also of Saul's experience on the road to Damascus:

> Suddenly a light from heaven flashed around him. He fell to the ground and heard a voice saying to him, "Saul, Saul" (Acts 9:3-4).

For most of us, a sudden experience of transcendence or the supernatural will not reflect the full vision as experienced by Ezekiel or Paul. It may signal only one awakening aspect of the divine-human encounter. But it is nothing to fear. We need a lot more intelligent, informed, Christ-centered guidelines from our churches.

Do I give myself regular "Sabbaths"? Even if we achieve well-balanced work schedules and limit our professional and emotional demands, we still may experience exhaustion if we are not intentional about our regular personal Sabbaths.

For example, each hour we need tiny Sabbath *moments* of inner renewal: gazing at a sunbeam on the floor, looking at a beloved painting, smelling a flower, touching a leaf, listening to a bird, stretching and breathing deeply, holding our hands under running water, gently palming our eyes, or just quietly sensing God's breath upon and within us. Such tiny but powerful Sabbath moments are especially important after intensive thinking, working, or interaction with other people.

Each day, we should lay aside at least one *hour* of Sabbath time to be and do what delights us most. We might walk, enjoy a garden, listen to music, read a delightful book. Whatever we choose, we should do it with joy, not compulsion. God is present with us in these moments of personal delight as much as when we are praying.

We need one *day* a week for relaxing, joyous, humanizing activities. The original scriptural concept of Sabbath was not that of heavy church responsibilities or even of intense prolonged prayer. Originally it was given as a day of total peace and relaxation; a time to enjoy God's presence, knowing God also rested after the intensity of creation. The act of resting is a holy act.

We need a *week* each year (not the regular family holiday) when we can go off alone or with a few like-minded friends or spouse for a quiet retreat. It need not be a time of intensive reading or contemplation but a time of walks, music, drawing, sleeping, keeping a journal—whatever refreshes and renews us most deeply.

Hearing about other Christian leaders' experiences and celebrations of Sabbath is both interesting and helpful. One minister told me she leaves town the night before her weekly day off, so that the next morning she is already within her ambience of rest. An active church laywoman I know takes her hour of refreshment and delight first thing in the morning when she writes poetry of thanksgiving.

A pastor told me that he walks at least once a day to a nearby Catholic chapel where he sits quietly breathing in the peace of Christ's presence, gazing at the votive candle by the Reserved Sacrament. (Many Protestants find this practice helpful, including myself.)

Another lay leader prepares a fresh vegetable drink each day and walks slowly through his garden for half an hour while sipping it. One busy conference executive keeps a cassette player in her office. Once a day she closes her door, puts her feet up, and listens to her favorite music for half an hour! Another pastor enjoys walking, resting, or playing tennis with his wife during his quiet hour. He feels, quite rightly, that marriage is as holy a commitment as is ordination.

Yet another lay leader sits quietly at her table after breakfast, a candle lit, reading a few scripture verses, and inwardly talking with God about the events of the day ahead. A Christian businessman schedules a half-hour appointment with himself each day (writing the date in his appointment book) and keeps the date as definitely as if he were meeting a colleague. He takes himself for a walk, talks with God, sits down with a book, or opens the window and breathes the fresh air. Sometimes he takes out his collection of cartoons and gives himself the good medicine of hearty laughter.

One pastor told me that for fifteen years he has met with an ecumenical group of other ministers once a year for five days. They pray together, talk together, laugh together—balancing times of togetherness with times of solitude.

We need to take responsibility ourselves for our Sabbath times with unapologetic firmness and clarity. Though we have a right to expect compassionate respect and concern for our well-being and needs from our colleagues, friends, spouse, congregations, synods, and conferences, I believe that Christ also says "Feed my shepherds" to each of us personally. We are beginning to understand self-care in Christ's name as a holy act, not only as stewardship to God's "temple" within us but as deep witness to the faith that we are God's beloved. We are not instruments or slaves. We are the friend, the child, the spouse, the close, the dear one in God's heart.

"Take, eat, this is my body...." To take is as necessary as to receive. They are equally important, but they are not the same. And both acts are as holy as giving.

I offer six suggestions for the prevention and healing of spiritual fatigue. They all may help you, or perhaps only one will be right for you at this time. I do not know who first invented the phrase "soaking prayer," which is my first suggestion, but I find that it is one of the most helpful.

MEDITATION AND PRAYERS

Then the Lord said to Moses,
"I am going to rain bread from heaven for you,
and each day the people shall go out
and gather enough for that day" (Exod. 16:4).

Soaking Prayer

Lay aside all intensive prayer and reading. Lay aside intercessory prayer for a while. (God will take care of those for whom you pray as you rest.) Make your body comfortable and at rest, whether on a bed, a deep chair, on the floor, or on the ground.

With thee is the fountain of life:
in thy light shall we see light (Ps. 36:9, KJV).

Think of God's warmth and light surrounding you, as if you lie in the sun or a pool of water. If this image seems too warm or confining, think of yourself in a cool, blue lake or lying on the beach with the ocean waves gently washing over you. Or you may wish to think of yourself as an underwater reed, slowly swaying in the water currents, or as a flexible tree rocking in the breeze. Some other image may come. You may wish to let your own body slowly and gently rock from side to side as if you were being cradled.

Or you may just wish to lie very still and let God's light and breath flow slowly and deeply into every part of your body, saturating you just as water saturates a sponge. Your whole self is washed in God's presence.

This prayer can last for fifteen minutes or for several hours. Let it send you into sleep if you wish.

If you are seriously fatigued or ill, let this be your only form of prayer for a while—maybe for weeks. I have known people who were healed of illness while using this form of prayer. I strongly advise at least a few minutes of this form of prayer each day to prevent exhaustion.

Bodily Prayer

After a few minutes of soaking prayer, lay your hands gently on your heart, your abdomen, your forehead, or over your eyes, and inwardly (or aloud) pray slowly with pauses after this manner:

> The living love of Jesus Christ now fills me…
> calms me…heals me…renews me.…

You can touch or just think of any part of your body in special need and pray this prayer of Christ's indwelling presence. Use any words that you feel are right for you.

Breathing Prayer

> He breathed on them and said to them,
> "Receive the Holy Spirit" (John 20:22).

As you rest your body, think of your breath flowing in and flowing out. Let each gentle breath (do not force it) become for you God's breath of life breathed into you. Let the Holy Spirit, the Comforter, flow into your body like light as you breathe. Think of the rhythmic motion of ocean waves, the rhythm of your own gentle heartbeat.

Think of each painful, tired, or stressed part of your body as breathing in and out God's breath, as if each painful part had its own breathing organs. You may wish to touch this body part as it breathes in God's light.

Special Prayer Words

(This helpful approach is featured in Basil Pennington's *Centering Prayer* and Ron DelBene's *Breath of Life: A Simple Way to Pray*.)

Choose, or let form within you, a word or a short prayer phrase that helps you focus best on God's presence or that expresses your own deepest need or longing.

If a single word, it could be something like *peace, release, God, Jesus, Spirit, light*. If a phrase, it could be "God, I need to feel your closeness" or "Jesus, fill me with your light" or "Holy Spirit, breathe upon me"—short, rhythmic phrases that say what you feel. Let this special word or phrase go through the day with you, becoming a central pool of peace and strength for you. Eventually you may find the prayer spontaneously changing as you change.

Parable Walk Meditation

Set out on a walk alone with no special agenda or goal. Walk slowly, and ask God to show you something on the walk that you need to hear, see, smell, or touch. You will know the sign when you encounter it. It will have a special meaning for you and will be significant for you at this time in your life.

The special sign or message may be seen in a tree's shape, the sound of a bird, or a fragrance that awakens a memory. The significant sign may come through a child's voice. It may come through the feel of a flower petal or tree bark. It may come through the sight of a special house; the face of a passerby; or the sight of a cat, dog, bird, beetle. Whatever the sign, it will have a personal meaning for you: a memory that needs healing or one that brings refreshing joy, a simple gift of renewal from God, a sudden delight or laughter, the thought of someone who needs prayer. Whatever the sign and its meaning, you will recognize it as God's special word for you today.

Walking while praying is much more helpful for some people than lying down or sitting still.

Receiving Sacramental Food from Jesus the Christ

This meditation was a bit startling to me when I felt it first inwardly suggested, but it has become for me one of the most healing and empowering prayers of all. I don't wait until I am exhausted; I enter into it almost every day.

Think or picture yourself at the table of the Last Supper or with the disciples on the shores of Lake Tiberias. Think of or picture Jesus pouring out the wine, breaking the bread, and bringing them to you personally, giving them to you.

Or let the Christ bring you the bread and the cup right in the room where you are now. Receive these nourishing gifts from his hand with love and thankfulness, taking all the time you need, knowing that the deep sacramental bonding continues unbroken through the centuries between the risen Christ and each of us.

The envisioning of this nourishment can be a powerful intercessory prayer for another person or even a whole community as we picture or think of Jesus giving that person or that communal body the bread and cup of life.

Of course, the sacrament of Communion in church was meant to be a service of healing, restoration, and renewal. In times of deep physical, emotional, or spiritual fatigue, I suggest receiving this sacrament as often as possible. As it is given, sense the powerful and loving energy streaming into your heart and body. If you are in deep prayer for some person, bring him or her with you in your thoughts and heart to the Communion table.

> In confidence of Thy goodness and great mercy, O Lord,
> I draw near, as a sick person to the Healer,
> as one hungry to the Fountain of Life,...
> a creature to the Creator,
> a desolate soul to my own tender Comforter....
> Thou art willing to give me heavenly food...to eat,
> which is indeed no other than Thyself the Living Bread.[6]

8

---·❦·---

Our Deepest Flaw,
Our Greatest Gift

"Simon…, do you love me?"
(John 21:15).

S IMON PETER, WHO LOVES JESUS, denies he knows Jesus three times there in the high priest's courtyard after Jesus' arrest. How can this have happened? I, like most of us, have always been taught that these denials, so apparently out of character, rose from a sudden terror that Peter did not know he had—a sudden failure of courage. I took this approach for granted in my preaching, teaching, and writing. But a few months ago, when rereading the stories of Jesus' arrest and trial, I suddenly saw a wholly different scenario. For the first time, I recognized Peter's three denials of Jesus not as acts of fear or cowardice but acts of misguided courage!

All along, the Gospels make it clear that Peter is a brave man. He has his faults, but cowardice is not among them. He is the first to take risks, to do the bold, impetuous dangerous thing, such as leaping into the water to swim to Jesus or drawing his sword in Gethsemane to defend Jesus against the armed temple guards. After the arrest, he follows Jesus into the very courtyard of the high priest, up to the bonfire where other guards are stationed. He stands there talking to them, pretending to be an uninvolved bystander. He is taking terrible risks, which none of the other disciples dare to take. It seems so clear to me now, for the first time in my life, that Peter is desperately hoping he can do something, even now, to save Jesus. Obviously, if Peter were identified as one of the disciples, he would be arrested too, thus ending his ability to do something to help Jesus. So when accused, of course Peter denies knowing Jesus, hoping to remain anonymous until he can find some way to act.

Jesus must know exactly what is in Peter's brave, loving but stubborn heart as he watches him there, boldly sitting among the soldiers, trying so desperately to find a way to save his friend and leader. So often before, Jesus has known Peter to resist, to misunderstand, to define and control a situation. So often Peter has believed that he knows what is best for others.

For example, though Peter is the first to name Jesus as the Messiah, the Anointed One (Matt. 16:16), just a few verses later he totally resists the idea of the Messiah's inevitable suffering. He misunderstands again on the Mount of Transfiguration when he wants to build a permanent shrine there to Jesus' glory (Matt. 17:4). He misses the point yet again and resists Jesus' attempt to wash the disciples' feet at the Last Supper (John 13:8). And even after Jesus' long and loving explanation of what is to come and why he, Jesus, chooses it freely, Peter still thinks he knows best and draws his sword in the garden (John 18:10).

Then come the denials, rising out of this same root of stubborn, controlling love. And as Luke so poignantly puts it, "The Lord turned and looked at Peter" (Luke 22:61). That look breaks Peter's heart. Does he at last realize that he has, with the best intentions, tried to force events into his own agenda? Does he at last begin to understand that Jesus does not want to be saved through force and deception and that this is not the way God's kingdom will come on earth?

Peter weeps bitterly. Does he realize that he has grieved Jesus' heart yet again? Does he weep, knowing there is nothing he can do to save Jesus, nothing that Jesus will permit him to do? Is this why he does not stand at the foot of the cross with John and the three Marys? Perhaps he knows that if he were there when they hammer the nails into Jesus' hands, he would try again to do something forcible. His love is not yet the love that can just stand nearby, silently sharing the pain of the beloved. Perhaps he thinks the best thing he can do, given his nature, is to stay away. His shame is deep and terrible.

Jesus had recognized in Peter the flame of love that would

enable Peter to be the "rock" of the church. This strong warmth comes down through the ages to us today in its fire, its humanness, its risk-taking enthusiasm, its heartfelt commitment.

But Peter's central gift of fiery, empowered love needed healing. The dark shadow side of fiery love is a controlling possessiveness that judges what is best for others and tries to force them into that agenda. This controlling possessiveness has been the dark flaw of the Christian church through the ages!

For each of us, our greatest gift is always potentially our most destructive power. "Be careful lest the light in you be darkness....If then the light in you is darkness, how great is the darkness!" Jesus said in gravest warning (Luke 11:35, RSV; Matt. 6:23, RSV).

When the risen Jesus draws Peter aside, mercifully apart from the others, and asks him three times, "Do you love me?" I believe Jesus is not only healing Peter's memory of shame over the three denials; I believe Jesus is also healing Peter's greatest but misused gift: his fiery, courageous love. Jesus holds that supreme but flawed gift in his wounded hands; Jesus comforts and then gently but radically heals.

Three times the grieving Peter affirms his love. However, according to the Greek translation, significantly he still does not understand the *agape* meaning of the word *love* that Jesus uses. Peter continually responds that he has a brother's love for Jesus. His understanding of love is still somewhat limited.

Jesus responds to each of Peter's affirmations of love with the mandate to feed the sheep. He knows that as Peter's gift of love receives healing, Peter will no longer force his own will on others but will use that power of love to feed the hungry sheep of the world.

Then follows that strange allusion to Peter's own future:

"Truly, I say to you, when you were young,
you girded yourself and walked where you would;
but when you are old, you will stretch out your hands,

and another will gird you
and carry you where you do not wish to go"
(John 21:18, RSV).

The text tells us that this verse indicates the death Peter will die in martyrdom, stretching out his hands on a cross. But within the former context of agape love, I wonder if the text might also mean that Peter increasingly will abandon his agendas, his need to control, and his dependence on self. Stretching out one's hands is a gesture of openness, a gesture of receiving as well as giving. Perhaps Jesus is thinking of the time when Peter, in his usual bold risk-taking style tried to walk on the water to meet Jesus and began to sink. "Jesus immediately reached out his hand and caught him" (Matt. 14:31). Peter would learn through his healed power of love to stretch out his hands in many ways. He would learn the act of release through love.

To be girded (clothed) and carried in directions you would not choose for yourself might also be metaphors for receiving the care of others when you would much rather do everything for yourself. Allowing others to help requires deep self-release, deep humility. All along, this controlling tendency has been the stumbling block of Peter's personality. He does not want to stretch out his feet, for example, so Jesus can wash them. This stumbling block is the shadow side of his gift of loving. He always wanted to be the giver, the controller.

These verses that reflect on Peter's death also reflect the vision of the open and released life he will learn to live. We reflect the way we live in the spirit with which we die. We cannot divide the two.

The significance of this story of the great "rock" of the church is a profound one for all of us as Christian leaders. Every one of us has brought a special central gift into our ministry. Some have brought several gifts, but most of us sense a major one that is closely related to the core of our identity and our basic personality type.

In one of my earlier books I developed the biblical metaphors of the gold, frankincense, and myrrh—brought as gifts to
the baby Jesus—as categories of the gifts God brings to *us*.[1] As
our healing deepens and our inner empowerment expands, we
grow somewhat into all these categories. But we probably still
find ourselves rooted primarily in one of them.

The *gold,* the ancient symbol of sovereignty, authority, and
empowered leadership, may symbolize the radiant inborn gift to
inspire and evoke the enthusiastic cooperation of others. Here
we find the innovators, the builders, the organizers, the rulers—
all creative leaders.

The *frankincense,* an ancient symbol for the priestly role, for
the one who delves into mysteries, explores the unknown, who
connects the human and divine, today may symbolize those specially gifted in research, teaching, innovative thinking; skilled in
discernment and articulation. Here are the gifted teachers, scien-
tists, educators, theologians, liturgists, preachers: those who build
bridges between the mystery of God and the human condition.

The *myrrh* was (and still is) an anointing and healing oint-
ment extracted from a shrub that grows widely in the Middle
East. It could well symbolize those gifted in healing, compassion,
and sensitive intuition. Here are those who are especially enabled
to listen, comfort, counsel, and heal—a great gift.

But, as with Peter, our great inner core gift becomes the
darkest, most destructive force within us if that gift is wounded,
abused, misused, or stifled. And the reverse is equally true. Our
inner stumbling block, our darkest inner flaw can become again
our most central and radiantly empowered gift when healed. In
chapter 3, I reflected on the abusive approach to spirituality
with its counsel to break down, throw out, rip out, or kill our
ego-centered inner flaw. This approach is not only abusive but
also useless. Nothing can kill our central empowered gift that
comes from God's own hand, no matter how abused or twisted
it becomes. Therefore we can give up those retreats (I used to
lead them!) in which we write our worst fault on a paper and

cast it into a fire! We can stop our pleas to God to pull out or execute our central flaw. Instead, as with the example of Jesus' encounter with Bartimaeus (see chapter 4), we can encounter our deep inner flaw and ask it (in Christ's presence), "Who are you? What is your need? What is the wound that twisted you? What is your empowered gift? What might you become when released to God's hands and healed?"

The response of our inner self to this healing is quite miraculous. Infected destructive anger can become the clean empowered hunger and thirst for justice. Our fear and anxiety can become sensitive empathy for others. Our manipulative dominance can, as with Peter, be healed into creative, loving leadership. We can begin to view our lethargy, our inertia (the *accidie* that the mystics often experienced and warned against) as the hopeless depression that sometimes is the dark side of the genuine spiritual flame. God's healing of our sensuality and greed can transform them into our loving embrace of this world.

We need, of course, to look for the face below the face of our central flaw. Often anger masquerades as fear and fear as anger. Often manipulative dominance or compulsiveness covers up a shy, frightened inner self. To discern the true face and name of our central flaw requires "truth in the inward being." We may need the help and discernment of a trained counselor in this process.

The point is that nothing that truly *belongs* to our personality can be destroyed. Some inner problems, such as emotional burdens we have internalized from others in our communities, do *not* belong to us. (I will reflect on this further in chapter 9.) But that which is innately ours will be with us always, for better or for worse.

I am appalled when I remember what I wrote twenty-five years ago: that spiritual self-examination is like an x-ray of a diseased organ held up to the light, so that we may see what needs to be cut or burned out! I did not know any better. I passed along what I had received from others.

Now instead, I think of an ancient religious ceremony in which the celebrant stood at the portal of the temple each morning. As the sun rose, the celebrant lifted a cup of wine to the rays of the sun. This cup symbolized all the twisted destructive powers of the peoples of the world, now lifted to the purifying sun, the heart of God, so that they might be transformed into healing energies.

Healing and transformation are far more radical (meaning pertaining to roots) than is destruction. When God heals and transforms our major flaw into what God meant it to be—our greatest empowered gift—then we say with the psalmist:

> The stone that the builders rejected
>   has become the chief cornerstone.
> This is the Lord's doing;
>   it is marvelous in our eyes (Ps.118:22-23).

REFLECTION AND MEDITATION

> These are the words of the Lord God:
> Now I myself will ask after my sheep
> and go in search of them....and rescue them,
> no matter where they were scattered in dark and cloudy
>   days....
> I will search for the lost,
> recover the straggler,
> bandage the hurt,
> strengthen the sick,
> leave the healthy and strong to play (Ezek. 34:11-12, 16; NEB)

Rest your body in a comfortable position. Take a few deep, slow breaths; then let your breath become light and gentle. Reread these verses from Ezekiel slowly, either silently or aloud. How do they seem to apply to you?

Which of your inner "sheep," your gifts and powers, do you feel have wandered off, become sick, weak, wounded, or more powerful and dominant than the others? These are the very ones that God's own self seeks and enfolds with love.

Has a particular gift or power become a problem? Can you name it or make an inner picture of it? Does it show itself through anxiety, fatigue, anger, inertia, or in some other way?

How does this flawed inner gift affect your daily life? the people closest to you? your ministry?

Ask the risen, living Christ, who came to fulfill rather than destroy, to be close to you as you look at or think about this particular inner flaw. You have often condemned this part of yourself, rejected it, even while often surrendering to its destructiveness. But the living Christ has seen and understood more deeply.

When you feel ready, picture or just think of Christ the Healer asking your inner flawed one to share how it feels and what it needs. Perhaps it can begin to understand and express how it became so flawed. But if unready, for now simply know that the flawed one is consciously in the Healer's presence.

When you feel ready, think of or picture the Christ, that great shepherd of the sheep, anointing your deepest inner flaw with healing, sacramental oil—just as earthly shepherds anoint the wounds and bruises of their sheep.

Picture or think of Christ, the Good Shepherd, saying as he anoints your inner flawed one:

> I anoint you in the name of God, the Holy One,
> that you may be healed, forgiven, restored, and released
> to your God-given light and wholeness.

Now move back from this inner part of yourself to your *whole* self. What do you feel happening between yourself and the Healer? Do you sense any change? Even if nothing seems to happen at once, remind yourself that the sacramental healing power is at work in the very root and core of your problem self.

You may repeat this inner anointing as often as you wish, just as any Christian is invited to come to a service of sacramental anointing and healing.

Rest and breathe quietly in the presence of the Healer, the Good Shepherd. Later, at another time, you may be able to embrace and reconcile with this deep part of yourself you have rejected for so long.

If not now, later you may begin to discern what deep empowered gift may lie within the flaw. If you feel ready to ask this question of the Healer (or even ask the problem self!) what gift it offers when healed, take special note of any inner word, symbol, picture, or memory that comes into your consciousness. The inner great gift may be speaking as it is released.

When ready, bring your meditation to a gentle close, becoming slowly aware of your bodily self and your surroundings. Stretch, yawn, gently rub your face (and perhaps your whole head), and your hands. Give thanks and give yourself a little more space and time before you return to your usual activities.

Verbal Meditative Prayer

If visualization makes you uncomfortable, you may wish to say a prayer rather than picturing.

Make your body comfortable; breathe a few deep, slow breaths; then let your breathing become light and gentle. Remind yourself you are in a safe place and that God's love surrounds you. You might wish to say inwardly or aloud:

"I thank you, God of love, within me, near me, around me."

Reread the verses of Ezekiel. Reflect on the meaning of this passage for you and your inner major fault.

When ready, lay your palms on your heart area (or whatever part of your body you choose) and close your eyes, or gaze at a picture that is meaningful to you or a cross or a flower or a view out your window.

Pray after this manner (or in other words that you feel God gives you):

Healer, Holy One, risen Jesus Christ, Shepherd of the sheep, Come with your full light and power.

Put your arms around this inner flaw, this problem self of
    mine.
Though I have rejected it and been ashamed,
You have always seen it for what it was meant to be.
Compassionate Shepherd, anoint my deep flaw with your
    holy oil.
May it be healed, restored, and released
to its health, strength, beauty, and God-given giftedness.
I pray this in your Name, through your Power, and by your
    Word.
I give thanks that the healing has begun.

Sit quietly, resting. Do you notice any change in the way your
body feels? As you close your meditative prayer, take two or
three deep slow breaths and stretch. You may repeat this prayer
at any time.

9

Spiritual Protection in Toxic Relationships

"Stay here in the city until you have been clothed with power"
(Luke 24:49).

ECENTLY A PASTOR WHO AS A YOUTH had lived near the oil fields told me about the "fire-jumpers." When scattered wildfires occurred near an oil well, firefighters wearing flame-resistant suits were dropped onto the burning grounds to clear the area and quench the fires before they reached the oil source with its steady, controllable flame. They wore the special flame-resistant garments to protect themselves.

As I listened to his description, I thought what a powerful analogy this situation was to so many forms of ministry, whether lay or professional. Sooner or later, we in Christian leadership will find ourselves in the midst of devastating human suffering, woundedness, and destructiveness. We will be very much in those "burning grounds," trying to encounter and heal the destructiveness and searing pain before they reach and quench the central living heart and hope of a person or communal body.

Each one of us, whether professional or lay, needs the flame-resistant clothing, the spiritual protection of Christ's light. We need to be, as the Gospel of Luke puts it, "clothed with power from on high." If we leap into the depths of human suffering without the awareness that Jesus leaps with us, if we enter the flames without the power of the encompassing heart of Jesus, we will become (as he warned us) dry branches. And the suffering we seek to heal will burn and perhaps even destroy us. (See John 15:6.) The much-used term *burnout* becomes very significant in this context!

My own theological training had not prepared me emotionally or spiritually for the draining, depletion, and burnout so often encountered in Christian leadership. In this generation, we are now at least learning how to recognize the outer signs of overwork, overextension, codependency. We are learning more about setting appropriate limits to protect our time and strength. But often we still do not understand how to recognize and protect ourselves from the silent, subterranean, *inner* draining and inner burning toxicity.

A wise, older woman minister taught me that the more one becomes open and sensitively intuitive through prayer, the more one also becomes open to the deep, unspoken levels of others' needs, expectations, projections, and darkness. In the same way, the more one is open to compassionate awareness for communal bodies and the pain of the whole world, the more one is also open, inwardly as well as outwardly, to the deep toxicity of unhealed communal wounds.

This realization seems unfair at first. If we are growing in spiritual compassion, why do we not receive automatic protection? Why does spiritual growth make us even more open to inner invasion? Why do healers sometimes die of the illnesses they have helped heal? Why do so many compassionate people succumb to fatigue and illness?

The only answer to these questions that occurs to me is that spiritual growth must include wisdom, discernment, and the intentional, deepened bonding with the heart of Jesus Christ as we move into risk and danger. Apparently good intentions are not enough in our three-dimensional material world or on any other level of reality. We need new spiritual maturity and intentional spiritual empowerment.

"See, I am sending you out like sheep into the midst of wolves; so be wise as serpents and as innocent as doves," Jesus said startlingly to his disciples (Matt 10:16). Wise as serpents! What an unexpected way to put it, considering the reputation of the serpent in scripture! Jesus continually used the unexpected, surprising metaphor when making a strong point.

The writer of Ephesians warns the church in Ephesus to put on the whole armor of God. This warning includes what we call demonic forces but is not limited to that aspect of destructiveness. By far, most of the daily inner assault and draining we experience comes unconsciously from the human beings around us and the communal bodies to which we belong. This inner draining and toxicity seems to happen in four major ways:

1. through the hungry need of another person or communal body;

2. through the projection or transference of another's expectation, longing, or hostility upon us;

3. through our own internalization of the problems or toxicity of others around us;

4. through the inheritance of generational problems from our family or other communal body that we have joined.

Draining. We may experience draining as sudden fatigue, wilting, chill, dizziness, sudden inappropriate anger, or anxiety. We may feel a need for more air, have a sudden longing to sleep or to eat or drink something sweet or stimulating.

As stated earlier, make sure that none of these symptoms is health-related. But if there is no apparent health-related issue and if these symptoms come in particular relationships (communal or individual), then perhaps others have latched onto our personal energy field and are drinking from it. Such persons are not necessarily selfish, egocentric, or outwardly demanding types. They may be gentle, inoffensive, and quiet. But for some reason they do not or cannot draw their vitality from God or from the lifestream around them, taking it instead from the nearest spiritual leader: pastor, teacher, counselor, chaplain, health-care giver, or anyone who represents a source of strength. They usually have no idea what they are doing, but the persons from whom they draw strength begin to feel wilted and irritable and long to get away from their presence.

As Christian leaders, we feel guilty about our reaction; there is no apparent cause for offense. We return to the next encounter determined to be kinder, more generous and giving. But the same thing happens: As we wilt, the person who drains us gains strength from the encounter, looking and feeling more vital.

Eventually such energy drain can cause health problems if we are in frequent contact with the draining person. This drain can also damage communal relationships. I have known more than one prayer group to disintegrate when one member drains the others.

Sometimes not one person but a whole needy community drains us of vitality. One woman told me she generally avoided family reunions. Nothing outwardly was said or demanded, but she felt that the group's hungry need was so deep that nothing she could do or say could ever fill it up. She would come away from each reunion completely exhausted.

Often we think this draining is our own inner problem. We believe that something about the other person triggers old associations and memories. Sometimes we think that we see our own less-than-perfect selves reflected in the other. Sometimes this perception is true.

But I think we can discern whether we have an inner problem of our own by asking ourselves these questions:

- Do I usually feel this way around other people?

- Are these symptoms and responses my usual way of responding to difficult situations?

- Do I react this way (with chills, dizziness, fatigue) when I encounter persons that I clearly link with troubling past associations?

- How do other people respond to this person or group?

- Do others often wilt or grow annoyed or restless when in the presence of this person or group?

Projection. When another (often without a word's being said) projects his or her desires, needs, self-image, or hostility on us, we do not usually have pronounced bodily symptoms. We are more likely to begin to lose our inner sense of stability of self. We may become confused about who we really are or what we really feel or want. We may lose the sense of borders and boundaries. We may feel that we need to act a part, live up to something, react in ways that are not typical of us. I like this explanation from Conrad W. Weiser:

> One of my former supervisors...said, "I look in the mirror every morning and I see myself. I know what I look like and who I am. When a patient begins to relate to me in ways contrary to that which I see in the morning, that is transference. When the patient begins to look different to me, more desirable, more repulsive or more like my brother, that is countertransference."[1]

A great deal of this transference or projection goes on even outside counseling or pastoral relationships. The usual sign is that we begin feeling or acting in ways unlike ourselves.

Internalization. The problem of internalization is the process by which we take into our own bodies or personal space the problems and darkness of others. The condition is related to the projection experience but is more generalized and diffused. It may involve a special relationship or a special community or a reaction to relationships in general. Its symptoms resemble those of being drained but are usually more gradual and chronic. We may experience unaccountable health changes, a growing fatigue, unusual dreams, emotional reactions that feel strange to us, a feeling of powerlessness and malaise, a generalized problem with boundaries. It is especially significant if these feelings are experienced after establishing a new relationship (such as a new counseling arrangement) or having begun special intercessory prayer recently.

We spiritual leaders endanger ourselves and others when in our prayers or teaching about prayer we urge *identification* with those for whom we pray. If we try in our thoughts and prayers to *become* the sick person, the hurt victim, the addicted, the imprisoned, the depressed, our bodies and emotions may obediently begin to take on the very symptoms and problems we are praying about! Therefore, in a workshop never ask the members to take into themselves the pain of the whole world. There is only One who can identify safely with the sick, the depressed, the addicted. Only One can take in the pain of the whole world! We are definitely not asked to take into our bodies and personal space the pain of the whole world in our loving, counseling, burden sharing, or intercessory prayer. We are asked only to become part of Christ's consenting community, helping to focus the power of his divine healing.

Inheriting or absorbing communal toxicity. This process is the one by which we have taken into ourselves, perhaps from birth, a specific generational, long-term communal pain and toxicity, whether of family, gender, race, ethnic group, or church. We may have been born into the situation, or we may have joined it through covenant or commitment. I have known several pastors who begin to notice strange symptoms in themselves after working for some months or years in a wounded parish, especially if the parish members have not openly faced and discussed those wounds, thereby allowing them to heal. I have known active lay leaders who have been affected the same way.

We all have known cases in toxic workplaces where both employers and employees become sick and unhappy. I have met both teachers and students who begin to feel the silent weight and darkness of certain educational institutions. And, of course, those who marry or come close to a deeply wounded family often begin showing many of the same symptoms of that communal body.

These signs indicate that we may have absorbed communal toxicity:

- Significant bodily changes, changes in eating and sleeping patterns, a general drop in immunity against illnesses, unexpected and rapid weight changes.
- Depression, anxiety, listlessness, irritability, or great restlessness that began after joining a community—possibly a distinct drop in self-esteem.

- A growing feeling of being trapped, powerless.

- Unusual escape dreams, such as running from burning houses, fleeing from tidal waves, being beset by robbers, trying to get out of mazes or complicated houses.

- Increasing addictive behavior, such as overworking, overexercising, overreading, obsessive interest in things that did not interest us before.

- A feeling of unreality about activities, friends, communities outside the toxic relationship in which we are involved.

- A growing desire to propitiate and meld into our community or a growing desire to make trouble, to rebel—or both.

- An increasing difficulty in understanding or expressing clearly our own truth: our needs, our feelings, our perceptions.

I need to emphasize that these possible symptoms as well as the others mentioned in this chapter might be due to onset of illness or clinical depression; if they continue or are pronounced, always check them out medically. But, as mentioned before, even if we discover illness, it is still appropriate to ask ourselves if we are in a toxic communal situation that may have lowered our immunity to the illness or may be making it worse.

We can be reasonably sure that we have been exposed to toxicity if our community is a group that has had severe trauma or woundedness that the members have never fully encountered or offered for healing. A high turnover of personnel, a high record of illness, emotional crises and/or inappropriate behavior can also indicate that our group has become toxic, and that toxicity may be affecting us. For example, a pastor wondering if a wounded church is emotionally and spiritually infecting him or her would be wise to find out how former pastors have reacted. How many became ill on the job, burned out, suddenly left, broke down, or became guilty of misconduct? What can be known about other staff members or long-term lay leaders? Are there communal scapegoats?

Make note if the community has a high level of secrecy with much whispering behind closed doors but little said openly. Frequent blowups and quarrels with no attempt to get at the underlying root problems are significant. The *unnamed* wounds and problems are the most toxic.

One problem with the absorption of communal darkness is that we often do not realize how affected, even saturated, we are by the poisoned atmosphere. The shadow can creep up on us so imperceptibly like gathering fog or deepening twilight that we cannot perceive that we *are* suffering. We begin to take the underlying darkness for granted. Our surroundings become the only reality.

This slow absorption of communal darkness is especially devastating for those who have experienced it from birth. As little children they simply did not know any other way of living. Having many healthy contacts and relationships outside our community or special friendships is vitally important. These persons can serve as reality checks who will "hold us honest" in clear thinking and truth speaking. (For a powerful and thoughtful guide for encountering toxic individual and communal abuse in congregations, see Note 2, chapter 9.)

As we reflect upon the corrosive problems of projection, internalization, and communal toxicity, it is vital that we avoid a suspicious, paranoid attitude toward our relationships and communal involvements. All too easily we fall into a "me-them" stance in which we perceive ourselves as the victim that everyone is out to drain, infect, or exploit. Those who drain us, those whose darkness we internalize, are wounded people who, for the most part, know not what they do. They are too wrapped up in their own pain to be aware of or overly concerned about their effect on other people.

I once counseled a professor in a theological school who felt deeply alienated, left out. No one responded to his gestures of friendship. People immured themselves in their offices with little interchange. There was hostility and suspicion between a faculty and an administration with strongly differing agendas and priorities. The professor noted that he felt increasingly sicker just walking down the halls. "The only thing that gets me through the day," he confided, "is to realize that as I walk down those halls I am among the walking wounded. I need to take a pastoral stance, like a chaplain walking down a hospital corridor."

Of course, we must ask whether staying in such an atmosphere is safe emotionally or spiritually. God sometimes calls us out of a community or relationship when it threatens to destroy us. God called Jesus out of Nazareth, his hometown community, when the community members rose up against him and tried to execute him (Luke 4:24-30). Such a call out is as valid and holy as God's call to go in.

Placed within the context of that particular chapter about relationships, I am convinced that Jesus' challenge—"If your hand or your foot causes you to stumble, cut it off and throw it away;…and if your eye causes you to stumble, tear it out and throw it away" (Matt 18:8-9)—refers to the necessary end of a destructive relationship. The biblical symbol of a hand means that which empowers us. The biblical symbol of an eye means that which enlightens us. We may enter into a committed relationship, intending to give and receive empowerment and enlightenment. Instead we find ourselves disempowered and our inner light destroyed. In such a case, anything is better than continuing the destructive bonding. But the pain of breaking the bond is as cruel a pain as a physical dismemberment.

If we feel called to stay in a toxic relationship as a freely chosen cross, we should acknowledge these signs and safeguards:

- We have made the choice in freedom.
- We have seen and named the toxic problem for what it is.
- We have learned about borders and limits, what is and is not acceptable behavior towards us.
- We have learned to tell the truth about ourselves: who we are, what we need, what we choose.

- We have learned to listen to the warnings and signals from our own bodies.

- We continue our own depth healing and explore the frontiers of new, healthful ways of living.

- We search for other people within the community who share our perceptions and with whom we can pray.

- We maintain healthy relationships with persons outside the community who share their truth and give emotional encouragement.

- We maintain an active, healthy life of prayer, knowing that the empowering love of Christ embraces not only ourselves but the whole community.

But we need not feel guilty or faithless if we feel the call of God to leave a communal situation. This is a holy call, no less than the call to remain. Sometimes the challenge to leave comes through a realization that our relationship or communal covenant is poisoning the very source of light and life within us, or when a new release and possibility opens before us that has a deeper authenticity for us, encouraging the unfolding of new gifts within us.

Some years ago on a sabbatical leave, my husband and I traveled to various shrines in Europe associated with legends of the saints. We were especially fascinated with the legends of Mary, Martha, and Lazarus. Those close and beloved friends of Jesus felt called to leave Jerusalem during the persecutions after Jesus' death—unlike Peter, John, James, and other disciples who remained in Jerusalem. To this day, many communities in southern France tell stories of how their little boat landed on the coast of what is now Provence.

Mary, Martha, Lazarus, and a servant woman each entered a special apostolate (a calling or special ministry). Mary became a contemplative in the coastal mountains; a contemplative order and a beautiful church were begun in her memory. Martha went further inland and tamed a dragon terrorizing a city. (That city still has yearly processions with a papier-mâché dragon in her honor!) Martha then became a famous preacher, converting many. We heard that Lazarus headed north to be a missionary to the wild Germanic tribes. Yet another legend reports that Lazarus became the first bishop of Marseilles and was later martyred.

The servant, a black woman named Sara, through the centuries became the patron saint of the Romany people. Many Gypsies from around the world gather each year to carry her statue to the seashore in a procession of honor. And as legend has it, Mary Magdalene also fled from Israel and, like Martha, became a valiant apostle in France.

None of this is scriptural, of course. But often old legends and traditions carry a core of truth. The point is that, within Christ's guidance, one can be in ministry whether staying or leaving, and God bestows the gifts of discipleship in either case.

I wonder if this is the essential meaning of the longer ending of Mark's Gospel when the resurrected Jesus says,

> "These signs will accompany those who believe:
> by using my name they will cast out demons;
> they will speak in new tongues;
> they will pick up snakes in their hands,
> and if they drink any deadly thing, it will not hurt them;
> they will lay their hands on the sick, and they will recover"
> (Mark 16:17-18).

Whether our mission is to stay or to leave, we will need the "new tongues" of love spoken in truth; we will need the gift of casting out infectious emotional and spiritual toxicity; we will have to encounter, touch, and even taste many threatening situations without being destroyed; we will need the healing touch—for some the gift of bodily healing, for all the gift of spiritual and emotional healing.

For all of us, this scripture passage warns of our need to learn how to live as empowered Christians in situations that carry potential risk. Even if God calls us out of a destructive situation, we will never in this world find any relationship or communal body totally free of conflict, challenge, threat. Martha met her dragon in France. The persecutors in Jerusalem were not her dragon, but the French dragon was.

To move back to the scripture story, the one specific cross that God invites us to bear does not destroy us. The one hundred fifty-three fish that God puts in our nets do not tear the nets (John 21:11). But if we do not wait for God's guidance, if we pick up every cross we see, if we load our nets with fish of our own choosing, if we take on every "dragon," then we are on the royal road to breakdown. The often heard but dangerous comment, "If I don't do this job, nobody will!" is a flashing warning light that someone (maybe ourselves) is about to over-load the net with fish that God has not sent. We do not experience spiritual protection when we "go faster than grace" as one spiritual leader (I think Brother Lawrence) expressed it.

Jesus prayed for us all the night before his death:

"I am not asking you to take them out of the world,
but I ask you to protect them from the evil one" (John 17:15).

I believe this comment refers to more than demonic power. I believe it also applies to the daily toxicity, the draining, the internalization we potentially encounter every day in our Christian leadership.

You may wish to look again at chapter 5, which lists the signs of a true cross, and at chapter 7, which lists the signs of excessive fatigue that so often lead us into a victimhood stance. When it comes to the problem of the frequent draining we experience, the translation in the New Revised Standard Version of the story of the hemorrhaging woman helps me greatly in my understanding. When the woman touches Jesus' cloak, Jesus is immediately aware that power has "gone *forth* from him" (Mark 5:30, *italics mine*). This is a world of difference from earlier translations that say power *went out* of him. And it is far more than just a semantic difference. In our own lives as Christian leaders, we each have felt the profound difference between vitality and power going *out* of us and vital power going *forth* from us. The first implies a sense of depletion; the bleeding woman must have felt drained by her chronic, seeping hemorrhaging. Vital power continually went out of her. The second implies a flowing forth from an abundant source. Jesus certainly felt the motion of his vital energy, but the story does not hint that he felt depleted and drained. On the contrary, not only did the woman receive healing, but Jesus went on to raise the daughter of Jairus from her deathlike sleep.

Saint Bernard of Clairvaux of France (1090–1153) is quoted as saying almost nine hundred years ago,

> If you be wise, you will make yourselves to be reservoirs rather than conduits [channels]…the former discharges all its waters almost as soon as received; the latter waits until it is full to the brim….Charity wishes to abound first unto herself *that she may also abound unto others (italics mine)*.[3]

This warning is not a selfish "me first." It comes from one of the most austere saints of history, who lived a life dedicated to the needs of others and saturated with the joy of the living Jesus Christ. It is a warning of the most profound and realistic wisdom: We cannot give to others that which we ourselves do not have. If we have not entered into the inner abundance that God has promised us, we cannot lead others or share that abundance with others. If we ourselves have not drunk from that overflowing cup of Psalm 23, we cannot lead others to that cup.

This was my own story, of course, as I shared in chapter 1. Early in my ministry, I had forgotten that the resurrected Jesus Christ is the vine, and I am the branch (John 15:1-5). My problem was as sad and simple as that. I was living my ministry trying to be the source, the vine, the fountain of healing love and endless vitality.

Even when I learned that the source is the living Christ, I

still made the mistake of thinking and praying as if I were primarily a channel (a "conduit" as Bernard calls it). I thought of myself as the go-between, fronting for Christ. I somehow had the inner image of Christ standing behind me and the persons to whom I was ministering in front of me, rather like an electric wire with God's power rushing through me to others.

Three problems arise with this image of ourselves as a channel or electric wire:

1. A channel of water can become contaminated if the toxic or contaminated earth into which it flows backs up. And the darkness of others can infect us if we unknowingly internalize their problems into our own bodies and space.

2. A channel gives out immediately what it receives without allowing time for its own healing immersion and transformation. (Bernard's point)

3. The whole analogy of a human leader or minister as a channel, wire, or instrument of any kind is alien to Jesus' understanding of the Resurrection relationship:

   "I do not call you servants any longer,
   because the servant does not know what the master is doing;
   but I have called you friends,
   because I have made known to you everything that I have
       heard from my Father" (John 15:15).

We are not in a mechanical relationship. We are in an organic relationship, a holographic relationship, *in which the whole is encoded and inherent in each of the parts*. In the union and communion of vine and branch there is an intimate wholeness of sharing. No distancing or separation exists between the source and that which it feeds and renews. God within the Christ enfolds and revitalizes both ourselves and the ones to whom we minister. In this way we experience sharing without self-shredding, vulnerability without "invadibility," empathetic imagination without internalization.

When I read the story of the Good Samaritan from this

perspective (Luke 10:25-37), along with many other fascinating aspects, the Samaritan's compassionate empathetic respect particularly impresses me. He gave the urgently needed help, though he knew he was possibly in danger from those same robbers; he handled a bleeding man, which many cultures considered ritually contaminating. He took the victim to the nearest inn and tended him all night. Then after promising to pay for any extra necessary care by the innkeeper, he continued his business trip. He did not lie down in the ditch, bleeding alongside the victim in the name of love. He got the victim out of that dangerous ditch! He did not abandon his own valid business to hang around the victim, nursing him indefinitely. Rather he delegated the on-going care to the innkeeper who was qualified for the job, and the Samaritan promised he would check back on his return trip to see how things were going.

The Samaritan respected the victim; he assumed the wounded man had the innate strength and desire to heal from his wounds and get back on his feet. He respected and trusted the goodwill and intelligence of the innkeeper. Finally, he trusted himself that he was doing his compassionate and practical best, but that he also had his own valid business and his own limits. He did not try to set up a permanent "helper-helpee" relationship with the one he had served.

This is not cold-blooded detachment. It may appear so to some at first because it has been so deeply impressed upon Christian leaders that we must become bleeding victims in our Christian service. Obviously we will sometimes bleed for others as we share their burdens and involve ourselves with their protection and release. Sometimes we have to fight for others. I'm convinced that if those robbers had returned to finish off the victim, the good Samaritan would have fought them off! (The wounded man was a helpless victim, unlike Jesus who had made a free choice and forbade Peter to fight for him.) Bleeding is also nature's healthy way of cleansing wounds and preventing infection. But there is a big difference between a brief, contained episode of necessary bleeding and the exhaustion of a chronic, draining seepage of blood.

Nothing in Jesus' teachings encourages codependence of any kind. I'm always a bit amused at that short, rather sharp interchange between Jesus and Peter after Peter's three avowals of love and Jesus' reflection on Peter's future. Peter notices that John is standing nearby. "Lord," Peter says, obviously indicating John, "what about him?" (John 21:21) Is this a flash of jealousy that John might not die until Jesus' return? Is it anxiety that John's form of future ministry and spiritual destiny may be a better, a more "spiritual" one? From John's perspective, are his feelings hurt that Peter is to "feed the sheep"? Does Jesus love Peter more?

There is a clean health about Jesus' reply to Peter: "What is that to you? Follow me!" The two disciples are bonded together in love and concern within the Resurrection relationship in Jesus, but Jesus clearly and cleanly separates them in their gifts, tasks, ministries, and spiritual destinies. Conrad Weiser reminds us:

> Professional detachment is the deliberate achievement of separateness in order to promote individual responsibility for healing. It is not the removal of the emotional self. Removal of self, on the contrary, is a move often taken by those professional helpers who are unconsciously afraid of connections;…essentially they are people who do not trust themselves.…Only when distance is maintained can the foundations of helping be built. On the other hand, distance without empathy is an empty space.[4]

I recall an instance of an older pastor who had become the enthusiastic counselor and prayer partner of an emotionally wounded woman in early middle age. Rather suddenly he became aware that he had lost the sense of space between the two of them, not only because of her needs but because of his own. Terrified at the possible consequences of emotional codependency, he severed the connection immediately. He refused to pray with her any longer and would no longer see, hear, or speak to her; he even refused to write her. He gave no explanation and gave her no referrals to another counselor or spiritual support system. His rejection almost destroyed her.

Apparently the pastor had been confused all along about healthy separateness among the loving members within Christ's body. He did not know how to build or maintain spaces. (I prefer the term "professional space" to that of "professional detachment.") He also was dangerously out of touch with his own needs, wounds, and limits. Certainly he was cruelly ignorant of the ways one might handle emotional transference by combining clear perception and boundaries with merciful concern.

One summer during my years of theological training, I took a job as secretary in the surgical department of a hospital. Bringing telephone messages to surgeons, I was often in and out of the operating rooms. On one occasion, a surgeon asked me to stand by for a few minutes until he could give a return message. For the first time I saw a surgically opened human body. I was astounded at the neat packaging of the human organs, each with its own strong, healthy linings that separated it from the other organs. A bodily organ cannot be in healthy harmony and cooperation with the other organs unless it is distinctly separate in its identity and function.

Paul makes the same point when he compares a human body to the church, the body of Christ. (Read 1 Cor. 12:12-27.) Each bodily part has its own task, but at the same time all parts have need of one another.

Our individual bodies and our communal bodies are full of polarity, which is not the same as polarization. Polarity connotes the same exciting vision as that of the prophet Isaiah (chapter 11) in which the different animals—opposites of all kinds—eat, play, and rest together while remaining in their unique identities.

This spiritual vision reflects the dynamics of our healthy Christian relationships. Our togetherness needs spaces and distinctions. Within the Resurrection relationship, our spaces are honored as well as the roots of our bondedness. Since I no longer try to imitate Jesus but have learned to abide in that vine, I no longer see myself as a channel or connecting wire. Now I see myself as held in the holographic model in which the risen Christ acts within me and the other simultaneously. The healing, transforming presence does not run through me to others but exists already in me fully and in all others. The reality is present, but our awareness usually sleeps.

Sometimes it helps to picture Jesus between me and the other, giving us both the healing touch. Sometimes I think of Jesus' powerful image:

"My sheep hear my voice.
I know them, and they follow me....
No one will snatch them out of my hand"
(John 10:27-28).

I think of myself held in one hand and the person to whom I am ministering held in the other hand, both equally loved and held, but in separate hands. This preserves our distinction while keeping us from codependence or feeding off each other's energy.

If I sense that another person has formed an inappropriate or draining attachment to me, I inwardly visualize or just ask the Christ to remove, gently but firmly, that umbilical cord between myself and the other; then to plant the cord in God's heart where the deep hunger will be fed from the source. If I realize I have attached myself to someone else in a draining way, I ask the Healer to remove my cord from the heart of the other and put my own hunger and need in God's heart.

Do not confuse this draining attachment, which I call the umbilical cord, with the golden rays of love we exchange between our hearts in a healthy, mutually giving and receiving relationship. Some people can actually see these rays of love.

We don't need to make inner pictures if we don't find them helpful. We can just pray inwardly, either ahead of an encounter or during an encounter, "Living Christ, enfold the hungry need of each one of us. Let each of us feed from God, the source. Take this encounter into your heart and give us spaces in our togetherness. May we each honor the uniqueness of the other."

At the end of the day or after intensive work with others, I ask God to cleanse me of all that does not belong to me. If I have internalized the darkness or toxicity or illness of another person (or community) into my own body and space, I picture or just ask that all that does not belong to me be gathered up into the great golden sun of God's heart. Once there, these needs and wounded energies are out of my own body and held within God where they will receive healing and restoration. This is a powerful intercessory prayer for others as well as a personal cleansing.

The following reflection and meditation is long and deep. You may wish to experience its stages at different times.

REFLECTION AND MEDITATION

Violence shall no more be heard in your land,
    devastation or destruction within your borders

. . . .

but the Lord will be your everlasting light (Isa. 60:18, 19).

The river of the water of life, bright as crystal,
flowing from the throne of God and of the Lamb
    through the middle of the street....
On either side of the river is the tree of life...
and the leaves of the tree are for the healing of the nations
(Rev. 22:1-2).

Rest your body, and breathe slowly and deeply two or three times; then let your breathing become light and gentle. Think of the love of God near you, enfolding you. Rest for a while in this awareness.

When you feel ready, think of an experience in your Christian leadership when you felt your energy go *out of* you. What was the occasion? How did you feel bodily and emotionally when this happened? Did you experience depletion, depression, coldness, anger, anxiety? What were the later results?

Now recall an occasion in your Christian leadership when you felt power flow *forth* from you, as from an abundant inner source. How did it affect you at that time, bodily and emotionally? How did you feel later? What differences can you discern in the actual results of the two encounters? Had you prepared ahead of time for the encounter? In what way?

Think back to the depleting interchange when power went out of you. What do you think now would have helped you then?

Rest quietly as the Healer speaks to you, through inner words or inner thoughts or inner impressions or symbols. This may be as far as you wish to go at this time with this reflection.

But if ready to go on, think of some future, challenging encounter: a group meeting, a counseling session, a hospital visit, a necessary but dreaded confrontation, a meeting with someone who has drained you in the past.

Ask the risen Christ to go ahead of you to that place in the future, to prepare that place for you, to heal it, to fill it with light. Picture or think of how the healing light of that future place now flows back to where you are now in time. Breathe in that healing light of the future place, slowly, calmly.

When you actually get to that future time and place of the encounter, think of the welcome and strength that awaits you. Ask that an inner picture or special prayer be given you. The picture or prayer may come as a circle of light around you that nothing can invade. The picture or prayer may come as a sense of the Healer's standing between you and the other. Or you may feel yourself held in one hand and the other person in the Healer's other hand. Or is some other inner picture or thought given? Hold this picture or thought for a while and gently breathe its power and reality. Then release the future event to God.

When you feel ready, ask God to clear from your body and personal space all that does not belong to you, all that is not part of you. You might think of a powerful gold or white light pouring throughout your body and your personal space.

Or you might think of that shining crystal river that flows from the heart of God (Revelation calls it the throne of God), cleansing your own inner city. The river releases all that it carries off into the ocean of God's mercy.

Now ask that God's radiant light, God's cleansing river within you may be so intensified that the cleansing may happen continuously and spontaneously.

Rest and breathe the new freshness of your personal space and the revitalization of your inner spiritual immune system. This may be enough for you at this time.

If ready, inwardly sense or inquire if someone has established a draining attachment to you. If you sense such a depleting connection (whether recently or long ago but still with you) ask the Healer to remove this umbilical cord of the other fully (roots and all!) and to put it into God's heart for nourishment. Give thanks that this is happening.

Now ask that God plant new spiritual power and beauty in the place of the uprooting. You may wish to picture or think of a flowering bush, a tree, a spring.

Picture or just think of the golden light rays exchanged among the hearts of those who are in healthy, balanced relationship with you. Give thanks for this exchange of love that gives as well as receives.

Breathe with gratitude the new cleansed release within and around you. How are you feeling now? Do you notice any change in your emotional or bodily self?

Claim the full empowerment of God, perhaps as a great circle of white or gold light around you, radiantly filling your whole body and space. Think of the hands of the risen Jesus, the Healer, on your head as you hear him say the empowering blessing: "Receive the Holy Spirit."

When ready, make a gradual reentry, with light massage of face and hands.

10

❧

Spiritual Discipline or Spiritual Response?

"And remember, I am with you always"
(Matthew 28:20)

*I*F THE RESURRECTION RELATIONSHIP is the core of our Christian spirituality, then it is also the core of our spiritual daily discipline. However, I personally have real problems with the word *discipline*. I know it refers to discipleship, the stance of one who learns. I also know (and like) the way some persons translate it as "attentiveness." But when I use the word *discipline* in spiritual counseling, at a retreat, or to myself, I have to spend a lot of time and energy explaining what it does *not* mean.

Too often a good, basic word gets overloaded, associated through the years with the wrong meanings. The overloading can reach the point that our head knows the real meaning, but our bodily and emotional response is all tangled up with old, damaging inner pictures. When reflecting on a loaded word, we can ask several helpful questions: What comes to my mind, memory, and emotions when I hear this word? How do I instinctively react and respond?

For me, the word *discipline* brings back memories of loud school bells announcing the next class time. I find myself thinking of the three-minute egg timer on the basin to time my toothbrushing. I think of a summer camp where we lined up each morning for fingernail inspection and the daily cabin check to make sure our beds were made up with square corners and the shoes were in order under the bed.

Undoubtedly these experiences—these daily disciplines— were excellent character builders. I do not resent or regret those drill routines. But I do not want to associate with the ultimate "lover of my soul" in this way!

I have the same problem with the words *methodology, techniques, practices, exercises*, and *training* as they relate to my spiritual life. For me, they have a routinized, mechanical, almost depersonalized feeling. They are certainly useful words to describe aspects of developmental competencies: learning a language or a sport, cooking, sewing, writing, or any other learned skill. They might apply to learned communication skills: how to listen, how to articulate what we feel and think, how to handle conflict.

But on a long-term basis, the way we relate to God, ourselves, and others was never intended to become a matter of techniques and methodologies. Even our bodily selves should not be treated in merely a technical way. Perhaps this is one of the reasons we so often fail in our physical fitness programs. A recent article by a nutritionist pointed out that if we call a new eating program a diet, it will eventually fail. We will almost invariably go back to our old ways of eating. But if we think of the diet as a whole new eating approach, and we learn more about what our bodies need for well-being, then we have not so much entered a program as a new way of relating to our bodies.

A friendship cannot last if we simply practice smiles and weigh every word before we say it. Sooner or later we have to move out into the depths of release and spontaneity by trusting ourselves and trusting the other. Our relationship with God was intended to be one of deepening trust.

For years I tried one method of prayer after another, and none of them lasted after my first enthusiasm. I feared I had to face one of two alternatives: Either I was not a spiritual person, or I was a lazy and undisciplined person!

But I could not accept either of these alternatives for long. I knew I was a person hungry for the spiritual life. I had been drawn into ministry by love of prayer and spiritual experience.

Nor was I all *that* lazy and undisciplined in my daily life. I was not a shining beacon of efficiency. I am seldom down to the wood of my desktop! But I had run a reasonably organized home with our small children. I had served pastorates and had held a variety of other jobs, not uncreditably, before my pastorates and maintained a complex schedule with reasonable success.

Eventually a third alternative occurred to me, something no one had ever suggested to me: *I needed to look at and take seriously my own natural way and rhythm of interpersonal response as significant for my prayer life.* I had always tried to imitate someone else's program, especially those of spiritual leaders both ancient and modern whom I admired. *Surely,* I thought, *if these methods worked for these holy men and women, then they would work for me.*

I knew better when it came to my personal relationships. I did not try to imitate other people's ways in my marriage, motherhood, or friendships. I read books about these relationships, took from them what I found helpful, and then developed my own approach taking into consideration my own instinct and my own personality type. But when it came to matters of the spirit, I allowed the experience and program of the leader or author to overawe me. I felt a keen sense of inadequacy when their methods did not work for me.

I had forgotten the intensely personal nature of my early experiences with God. The basic dynamics of a relationship with God are essentially the same as with any other depth relationship, though of course much more so. A depth relationship requires regular, honest, vital sharing. Without dependable, regular sharing, any relationship will starve and wither. But the *way* of this sharing—its timing, its rhythm—is unique to each relationship.

Somehow the idea had been deeply ingrained in me that I had to enter into prayer at the same time every day, in the same place, and for the same length of time. Also rooted in my subconscious was the idea that prayer ought to develop along the same order every day: adoration, thanksgiving, confession, petition, intercession, and commitment. Most of the books I read assumed this approach. But I do very few things at the same time and place and in the same order every day. And I certainly do not maintain my relationships in this way.

In my most fulfilling relationships, the love and sharing is daily and dependable, but the ways I show the sharing love are not always the same. Some days I like to sit down for long, intimate, focused conversation; other days I want to have spontaneous exchange with the loved one while doing dishes or walking or driving. Sometimes I like to sit in silence with my husband, and other times each of us does his or her own thing with a close awareness of the other.

Sometimes we like to leave home and be together—away from daily responsibilities, focusing on each other from a different perspective. Sometimes we engage in a season of intentional, intensive exchange at a special time.

Once I applied my personal rhythm of response to my prayer life, I felt a profound sense of release and relief. Not only did I naturally respond to God's love from the rhythm of my own way of relating, *but now I had found the way that would last a lifetime!* My own natural "discipline" was deeply planted in my own inner uniqueness. I had just never bothered to look at my uniqueness and respect it. I did not have to "take on" or "enter into" anything. I had only to observe the way my most fulfilling relationships worked and respond in that way in my relationship to God.

For me, this new approach meant that I could pray sitting down and meditating in depth, or I could talk to God spontaneously through the day. I could pray for five or ten minutes instead of an hour. It was all right if I prayed after lunch or late in the evening instead of before breakfast. I could walk in silence with God, listen to music with God, or exercise or dance in my living room with God.

Sometimes I left my daily responsibilities and went somewhere else to be with God. (Call that time away a retreat.) I discovered enrichment by setting aside several weeks (such as Lent, Advent, or some other designated period) for a structured meeting with God at the same time and in the same place. But knowing myself, I would not try to turn this structure into an everyday pattern.

Likewise, I released myself from the feeling that I had to talk to God using the same order of subject every time. Sometimes I would begin with a cry or a surge of thankful joy or the admission that I felt dry and tired. I might begin by focusing immediately on some pressing problem or someone else's urgent need. Or I might just begin with some moments of completely relaxed "soaking prayer." The important thing for me is to be honest, spontaneous, and attentive not only to what I feel and need but also to what God is saying deep in my spirit. This approach, based on the kind of person I am, has been effective, deeply rooted, and permanent.

Other people respond differently than I. Many people (not rigid people at all) find that a more regular, structured approach to their prayer time better suits their personality. Praying at the same time and in the same place each day is deeply helpful and natural to them. Some choose morning and night, before mealtimes, perhaps using printed prayers from a book before they move into their own personal way of praying. Often they will pray for others from a carefully prepared list and will offer this intercession at a special time each day. This approach to prayer fulfills and satisfies them; this daily structured order is not a strain for them to maintain.

I have noticed that these persons reflect this same structure and consistency in their personal relationships. They write letters at the same time of day, make their personal phone calls on a scheduled basis, and go out with friends at stated regular times. One of my most beloved friends (a most joyful, relaxed person) finds this approach to be her own true deep rhythm or response to God and to others. She does not define this way of relating as a discipline or methodology; this is just the natural way she lives and relates to others.

The point is that the only prayer life that will last through the years is the way that is rooted and grounded in our own unique *rhythm of response.*

Chester Michael and Marie Norrisey make clear the

essential connection between our temperament and our prayer life:

> All indicators point to a close relationship between our innate temperament and the type of prayer best suited to our needs. Introverts will prefer a form of prayer different from Extroverts. Intuitives approach God from a point of view different from Sensers....As we grow in maturity and learn to make good use of all our abilities in functioning and relating, our prayer life should become richer.[1]

As we grow and unfold, we sometimes appear to undergo a change in what we had thought was our basic temperament. In my opinion what we perceive to be a basic change is actually entrance into a deeper dimension of what we always were but did not know. New gifts, new potentialities wake up and come to the surface. If for much of our life a community mind-set has influenced us, if our families or our churches have put us into set categories that have moved us in directions that are not really natural to us; then new discoveries about ourselves will be especially disconcerting, unexpected—either exciting or threatening and maybe both.

Therefore, we must remain alert to new discoveries about ourselves and occasionally experiment, test the waters to see if God is inviting us to try out some new ways of spiritual life. We will probably notice similar changes coming about in the way we relate to other people. I don't think we can separate the way we relate to God and the way we relate to others. I like the way Marjorie J. Thompson expresses it:

> God's Spirit is continually challenging, changing, and maturing us....It can never be said in our lifetime that we have "arrived." The spiritual life invites a process of transformation in the life of a believer.[2]

As we remain alert to deep changes within us, we need to listen to our own responses, longings, and inner resistances and to respect what they tell us. If we feel unnatural, pushed, strained, guilty, then something is wrong about what is being suggested to us, whether by another person or by ourselves. If a new spiritual approach is right for us, it will feel natural; soon it will feel like a homecoming, even if some aspects offer a strange challenge for us at first.

As Christian leaders, we must ask pointed questions about our way of leading others into deeper spiritual life:

- Are we pushing others into the ways that work for us?
- Do we encourage others to look deeply into their own inner rhythms of response?
- Are we careful to explain that our own spiritual experience is merely that—our own experience and not a measuring rod for anyone else?
- Do we offer reading and workshop resources for those who wish to explore alternative insights?

Probably all that we do, even in our richest most effective sermon, lecture, workshop, retreat, spiritual guidance, is to remove the burdens and break the chains so that others may find release at last. We free others to explore, discover, and embrace that which has been within them all along—their own secret, sacred inner meeting place with God.

"I am with you always." This is the eternal source of our daily life of prayer. This is no technique. We are in deep waters of the most intimate of all possible relationships that flow to us—forever fresh and new—from minute to minute. And, as with all that lives, our relationship with the ultimate Person is organic, open-ended, unexpected, asymmetrical, and unfolding.

REFLECTION AND MEDITATION

> Before they call I will answer,
>> while they are yet speaking I will hear (Isa. 65:24).

For this meditation, I suggest you take whatever bodily stance helps you to think and remember. You may wish to take a walk rather than to sit down. You may wish to write your thoughts and memories.

But first take a few moments of quietness; a few slow, deep breaths, then relax your breathing. Reflect on your present way of responding to God in prayer. Try to remember, maybe writing it down, exactly what you usually do and how you usually pray. Be very honest. How long has this been your approach? How did it begin?

When you feel ready, ask yourself if this is the kind of relationship you have really wanted with God through Christ. If not, what do you sense is wrong? Do you feel that you are not growing? Have you become bored and resistant? Has prayer become an increasingly heavy duty for you? Do you find yourself trying to escape your times of prayer? Do you feel guilty or just resigned to these difficulties?

What do you feel is the cause of the problem? Are you trying to fit yourself into what you consider a spiritual mold? Did you have a preconception of what a strong prayer life "ought" to be like? Are you modeling yourself after someone else? Or is there some other problem?

When ready, ask yourself what sort of person you really are. What have your most fulfilling personal relationships been like? How have you learned to respond to these beloved people? Has there been a schedule? a special rhythm? What has worked for you on a long-term basis? What does this reflection suggest about your way of relating to God?

Now check your bodily relaxation (even when walking) and your gentle, regular breathing. Ask God, who hears us even before we speak and answers before we call, what might be a deeper, more living way to be in daily, loving communication. What might be richer ways for you, a unique person, to respond to God in a released, natural, spontaneous way? Don't focus now on what anyone else does, no matter how admirable. See what rises within *you*. Be attentive to inner pictures, symbols, special words. Remain alert for the next few hours and days for new perceptions to come flowing in. Give thanks that your relationship with God is already on a new and more vital level.

You might think of or picture yourself walking with Jesus or sitting across from him. Ask him as you might a beloved friend, "What can I do each day to respond from my heart to your presence? What is best and most real for me?" You may wish to ask these questions of the living Jesus Christ each day: "How can I best experience your transforming friendship today? What way can we best share and talk together today?" How do you feel like responding at this moment?

It may appear that each day will differ. Or you may feel the inner suggestion to have one main way of prayer for a period of time. Whatever suggestion surfaces will be in rhythm with the type of person you essentially are—because that is the person God created and loves.

11

Breath,
Bread,
and
Blessing

*Lifting up his hands, he blessed them
(Luke 24:50).*

E ARE TOLD IN LUKE'S GOSPEL that the risen Jesus led the disciples out as far as Bethany, where he gave them this special farewell blessing. Luke's Gospel is the only one that gives us this loving last scene at Bethany. Bethany is the hometown of Mary, Martha, and Lazarus—those close and special friends of Jesus and his disciples. This home often has been a warmly welcoming shelter for Jesus and the disciples. It has been a place for rest and shared thoughts. After the Resurrection, do they gather one more time at their friends' home? Luke does not tell us, but it is hard to believe that Jesus moves on into his deeper light and empowerment beyond human bodily vision (Ascension) without coming again to those three friends who had been so close to him personally and who had played such a significant part in his ministry. They are not among the special twelve; nevertheless, they are disciples in the truest sense. While only speculation on my part, I believe that Mary, Martha, and Lazarus are there to receive that loving blessing from Jesus', as yet, visible hands.

Even to that last visible moment and beyond, Jesus continues to feed the soon-to-be shepherds. He feeds them with renewal when he comes to the disciples behind their locked doors that Easter night and breathes on them the Holy Spirit. The Hebrew word *ruach* means "spirit" as well as "breath" and "wind." With this breathing of the Spirit, Jesus renews and empowers them to fulfill the great mandate to love and lift the burdens from others (John 20:19-23).

173

Jesus feeds two disciples with bread at the Emmaus inn and all the disciples beside Lake Tiberias later. Concerning the supper in Emmaus, the disciples tell "how he had been made known to them in the breaking of the bread" (Luke 24:35). Of course the disciples recognize him in these acts. They had often shared meals with him, those simple daily acts of bread breaking and bread giving. Some of his great miracles focused on the giving of bread. The giving of the bread had been the sacramental focus of the Last Supper as he shared with them the meaning of his decision to encounter the cross. All along, their associations with him included that deep nourishment, the "bread of life."

I wonder if Jesus, during his many significant acts of breaking and giving bread, sometimes thought back to the demonic temptation in the wilderness at the start of his ministry (Luke 4:1-4). Jesus was desperately hungry. I believe this hunger was not only of the body but also a hunger for ministry to the whole hungry world, which was starving physically, emotionally, and spiritually. He knew and felt his incredible powers. In the wilderness, he was tempted to use his powers to turn the stones of the desert into bread for himself—for everybody. Such a shortcut would have been simple, quick, and sensational. All three temptations offered opportunities to take a shortcut, to exercise his external use of power with the best of intentions.

But true bread comes from bread not from stones. Jesus made this abundantly clear when he accepted the loaves from the hungry crowd and fed the "five thousand men, besides women and children" (Matt. 14:13-21). He offered up his whole life as the living bread and said so to the crowd:

"The bread of God
is that which comes down from heaven
and gives life to the world....
I am the bread of life.
Whoever comes to me will never be hungry"
(John 6:33, 35).

Then Jesus gave the nourishment of the blessing. The biblical meaning of giving a blessing implied a special strength or energy given for a special task. A patriarch's laying hands of blessing upon his oldest son did not mean that he loved that child more than the others; but rather that the oldest son would need a special inspired strength when he inherited the responsibilities for the nourishment, safety, and survival of the family and tribe. (A curse did not mean the withdrawal of the love but the withdrawal of the special strength given for the task. The special strength was given to another if the person or communal group refused or abused the task.)

A pastor's lifting a hand to bless the congregation at the benediction signifies a special empowered strength given to the congregation to fulfill the great special mandate to love. When hands of blessing are laid upon the newly baptized or confirmed, the gesture is not just one of loving fellowship. It means that through the grace of the living Jesus Christ, the congregation focuses its prayers upon this person, and God's empowerment pours upon him or her as he or she enters the Christian life. When hands are laid upon those ordained or commissioned, it implies a special sacramental energy poured upon these shepherds for their various tasks.

The point of this book is not to separate the needs and nourishment of Christian leaders from those of Christians who are not in leadership roles at the moment. The breath, the bread, and the blessing are needed by all and given to all. A few years ago I experienced a unique Communion service in a highly liturgical denomination. As the priest lifted the bread and the cup, the members of the whole congregation stretched out their hands toward the bread and wine and said *with* the priest the eucharistic words: "Take, eat, this is my body broken for you....This is the cup of the New Testament in my blood. Drink ye all of it." The impact was overwhelming in its power. I thought, *This is the way* all *Communion services were meant to be!* Through the loving faith commitment of the whole communal body, which is bonded together within the risen Christ, the bread and the cup become for us the living sacramental presence of Jesus Christ.

But as I have stated throughout this book, that which is needed by all Christians is *urgently* needed by the Christian leader. In my counseling and retreat work among clergy and lay leaders, I encounter so many shepherds in their urgent need. Many leaders are so hungry that they constantly are tempted to take the many shortcuts of trying to turn stones into bread. We are *all* so often tempted that way!

A major aspect of this hunger is the widespread loss of ministerial identity. I recently talked with a minister shortly before his retirement who said sadly, "When I entered the ministry forty years ago, it was a profession full of significant tasks. We were not only respected by the community; we were *needed*. But so many of my former tasks have been taken over by other agencies. I feel my calling has broken down into little scattered, inessential jobs. I feel like a mere organizer now, just keeping my church together as an ongoing group. But for what? What is ministry anyhow? I don't know who I think I am any more."

This malaise is widespread. In earlier centuries, the church was the only center for the poor, the sick, the hungry, and the homeless. Originally churches founded and maintained all the hospitals, schools, and universities. The church was the place where great art was seen, uplifting music heard, and wise counsel given. The church was often the center of drama and storytelling, the church spire the tallest in town. Community members considered the pastor or priest to be the voice of God and the model of spiritual, moral values. In smaller communities the pastor or priest often was the only literate, educated person in the village and certainly the main dispenser of guidance and wisdom.

When I was ordained just forty years ago, the church in many small communities was still the social and cultural center. It was still the main place where neighbors gathered to share needs and concerns, where young people could meet one another and share activities. The pastor was still considered one of the major respected and informed voices, and his or her authority was something to be reckoned with.

Now, of course, business buildings tower above the church spire. Specialized professional agencies have taken over the tasks of education, health care, and social welfare almost completely. We don't need to go to church to hear voices of wisdom and guidance: They come from radio, television, newspapers, and the internet.

So what is left? Just busy work? What are we doing as Christian leaders that a professional educator, health or social worker, or community organizer could not do better? Many pastors throw themselves into one main aspect of ministry in an attempt to give meaning and significance to their lives: counseling, social justice, protest movements, liturgy, healing, meditation, and so on.

I don't deny that these avenues are often genuine apostolates for Christian leaders. Many of us see special and neglected aspects within the Christian community and feel called as Christian leaders to respond to those needs with vital joy. But I think all of us must necessarily ask the scary question: "Just what is my basic identity as a Christian called into leadership?" I'm not now speaking of the question of our personal identity, which is equally essential to ask, but of our leadership identity— whether professional or lay. We must ask this question *because* other agencies have taken over so many of our former tasks and definitions.

I would not want to return to the days when both we and the community viewed our leadership as the sole source of education, spiritual authority, cultural and communal gatherings, of solace for the poor and sick and ignorant. I am glad the wider community has gathered up these great missions. I think that is exactly what Jesus had in mind when he spoke of the yeast's eventually leavening the whole loaf.

My father, who died in his nineties, said that in spite of the world's continuing grave social problems, there is far more widespread compassion and social conscience now than when he was a boy and young man in the early years of this century. In those days federal or state social welfare did not exist. No laws protected abused children or laborers. We had no universal right to vote. There was little or no concern for the world's ecology. War was glorified. We took racial and ethnic separation and discrimination for granted. Environmental pollution was everywhere. Lynchings were common. "I would not want to go back to those days," he said. The spirit of compassionate awareness and concern definitely is spreading. It is no longer centered only in the ministry of the church.

Neither would I want to go back to the days when the roles of bread maker, clothes weaver, sole nurturer and health-care giver defined a woman's identity. When specialized agencies began to take over these tasks, many women for several uncomfortable decades tried to enrich their identity as housewives through more elaborate cooking, interior decoration, cultural and volunteer work. Some elected these activities with joy and fulfillment, but many others sensed a real emptiness and experienced severe identity loss. Finally women realized they did not have to be "housewives" in order to have a home. They could freely redefine and explore the alternatives of what it means to be a woman with a home. Nor would I wish to return to the concept of marriage as a survival unit of respectable social placement, economics, and procreation in which couples almost had to stay together, no matter how unhappy.

As the old definitions and necessities fall away, we are going through enormous communal turmoil while we explore the deeper meaning of marriage as a freely chosen covenant between two persons who commit their lives to each other for wholeness and well-being—marriage within God's shalom.

Likewise in the present period of history, Christians in

leadership are asked to reexamine and redefine the ministerial identity. This can be a frightening self-questioning as we move out of former concepts into new, deep waters.

We preach, yes, but that does not define us. We visit hospitals, teach classes, counsel, write books, lead retreats, but these activities do not define us. We work among the poor and champion social justice, but these acts in themselves are not our ultimate definition and identity. These acts are among our manifold tasks, but they do not in themselves become the core of our identity. What deeper roots underlie these activities? Who are we?

It is an exciting adventure to reread the scriptures, to reflect on Jesus' relationship with his disciples—especially within the Resurrection narratives—with this one question in mind: Who are we? In response, one major image and phrase kept surfacing for me: *We are the breathed upon.*

> Jesus said to them again, "Peace be with you.
> As the Father has sent me, so I send you."
> When he had said this, he breathed on them
> and said to them, "Receive the Holy Spirit"
> (John 20:21-22).

Recently I saw the movie version of C. S. Lewis's *The Silver Chair*, the fourth book in The Chronicles of Narnia series. One of the most powerful and symbolic scenes occurs when Aslan the lion (representing the Christ) sends the two children Jill and Eustace to Narnia to find and release the captive prince of that country. Aslan blows them there with his gentle, powerful breath. One at a time, they are held in the air and slowly blown over oceans, mountains, chasms, forests—sustained only by his breath. To me, this scene portrayed a marvelous image of ministry and of all Christian leadership. We too are the breathed upon; we are sent forth and sustained by the breath of that Spirit.

During my seminary days, we occasionally sang a hymn in chapel that I had never heard before and have never heard since:

I feel the winds of God today; today my sail I lift,
tho' heavy oft with drenching spray, and torn with many
a rift....
It is the wind of God that dries my vain, regretful tears,
Until with braver thoughts shall rise the purer, brighter
years....
Great Pilot of the onward way, Thou wilt not let me drift;
I feel the winds of God today, today my sail I lift.

—Jessie Adams, 1863

Even back then, this old hymn gave me an inner lasting metaphor of the wind, empowering breath breathed and breathing upon us—to do what?

To feed the sheep, says John's Gospel. To go forth into all nations, say Matthew and Luke's Gospels. To "go into the all the world and proclaim the good news to the *whole creation*" (Mark 16:15, *italics mine*) says Mark, astonishingly—to share the radical good news of new beginning and transformation.

These mandates grow from the one great stem of identity of the "breathed upon," the empowered. The bread and the blessing are of this same empowering sustenance for the shepherds.

I find it fascinating that the first empowerment given (according to John) as the Holy Spirit was breathed on the disciples was the ability to lift burdens:

"If you forgive the sins of any, they are forgiven them;
if you retain the sins of any, they are retained" (John 20:23).

But why was the power to release and retain sins the first gift to be breathed upon the disciples? Frankly, this verse was a stumbling block for me for many years. The promised gift seemed grim, scary, and unjust. How could any human being be given the power to bestow or withhold God's forgiveness and release? It took me a long time to understand the possible deeper meanings of this provocative gift.

In the biblical sense, to forgive means to release another

from the burden of a debt. Forgiveness releases the debtor from any expectation of repayment. Therefore, when God or someone in the name of God forgives sins, God closes the book of accounts, demands, debts, repayments, expectations, rewards, and punishments. We become a new creation. The burden is lifted. This understanding of forgiveness closely allies with Jesus' stated mission:

> "The Spirit of the Lord is upon me,
> because he has anointed me
>   to bring good news to the poor.
> He has sent me to proclaim release to the captives
>   and recovery of sight to the blind,
>   to let the oppressed go free,
> to proclaim the year of the Lord's favor" (Luke 4:18-19).

Every fifty years in biblical times, the Israelites were commanded to blow the shofar, the ram's horn, from atop the Temple walls in Jerusalem to proclaim the year of Jubilee, the "year of the Lord's favor," the year that was intended to be the year of universal release. (See Lev. 25:8-17, 23-55; 27:16-25; Num. 36:4.) Throughout the land, all slaves were to be freed, all debtors released from their debts. All land that had changed hands was to be returned to the original owners or their descendants. All arable land was to be given a year of fallowness and rest.

When Jesus proclaims this year of Jubilee and release in the Nazareth synagogue, he means that in God's eyes and in God's heart, the shofar of release has sounded within the land for everyone, even if this is not the official year. God invites everyone to enter this release and to be set free on every level. God wipes clean inner bondage, debts, guilt—personal or communal. All are set free to make a new start. *All* of Jesus' acts, words, miracles—his whole life—open prison doors and remove chains, offering release of every manner of communal and personal inner bondage.

A selection from one of the ancient New Testament apocryphal writings (possibly written as early as the second century) offers the following glorious visionary description of Jesus' descent into hell after his crucifixion:

> And: The Lord looked down from heaven
>> that he might hear the groanings of them that are in fetters...
> And now, O thou most foul and stinking Hell, open thy gates...
> The Lord of majesty appeared in the form of a [human]
> and lightened the eternal darkness
> and brake the bonds that could not be loosed:
> and the succor of his everlasting might visited us that sat in deep darkness...
> And lo, suddenly Hell did quake,
> and the gates of death and the locks were broken small,
> and the bars of iron broken, and fell to the ground,
> and all things were laid open....
> And behold, the Lord Jesus Christ coming in the glory of the light of the height,
> in meekness, great and yet humble...
> For behold, now, this Jesus putteth to flight by the brightness of his majesty
> all the darkness of death, and hath broken the strong depths of the prisons,
> and let out the prisoners, and loosed them that were bound...
> and the Lord set his cross in the midst of hell,...
> and it shall remain there forever.[1]

These words, like the sound of the shofar, blow throughout all our hells and prisons on every level. The empowered identity of all Christian leaders in their various roles is to blow that shofar, to sound that release.

We are called to sound the release through sermons or classes; through prayer and discussion groups; by the beds of the sick; on the mission field; among the homeless, the addicted, the despairing. We are called to sound the release through meetings of church boards, through religious publishers' offices, through financial drives, through church suppers, through pastoral home visits, through every word and act of the church. This full release was Christ's intention and promise and gift to the church. The release was meant to happen on every level—and yet, so often it has not happened.

Everything we say and do as Christian leaders has the effect of increasing or lightening the burden, tightening the chains around people's hearts and spirits or releasing them from those inner prisons. The grim warning within Jesus' empowered gift is the very real possibility that we may use our power not to release others but to retain the burdens—and even add to their weight.

All branches of the Christian church (with few exceptions) through the centuries have at some point added to the burden by increasing guilt, shame, heaviness. They have left unhealed the wounds and the generations of communal toxicity.

God does not refuse forgiveness and release just because a community or leader refuses. No human being can tie God's spirit down in that manner. But a burdened person (no matter how much loved by God) may go through life unreleased in his or her heart simply because the surrounding community does not proclaim the release, model the release, or witness to the release.

If we Christian leaders and our communities remain silent among the tombs, the chains, the prisons, the hells and refuse to enact the empowered release, the spiritually sleeping remain asleep, the spiritually trapped remain trapped until God's spirit breathes upon others who *will* sound the release in Christ's name. The spiritual leader is in a position to do almost indescribable harm among the vulnerable, the wounded, the abused in trust, the outcast, those trapped behind the bigotry of dividing walls. There are so many ways to "retain" those burdens, wounds, and hunger. And usually if we retain the burden for others, we have retained it within ourselves!

But often the great miracle happens, and a Christian

community and its leaders experience for themselves the lifted burden, the healed memory, the healed relationship, the release from the chains and tombs of old bigotries and dividing walls. And a Christian community or leader's experience of the mercy, freedom, and abundant sustenance of Jesus the Christ enables that community or leader to share the freedom and sustenance with all who come their way. The writer of Ephesians describes such a community, such a leader:

> Speaking the truth in love,
> we must grow up in every way into him who is the head,
>   into Christ,
> from whom the whole body, joined and knit together...
> as each part is working properly, promotes the body's
>   growth
> in building itself up in love (Eph. 4:15-16)

When we proclaim release and speak the truth in love, the Spirit transforms lives, heals bodies, gives hope, awakens and affirms gifts, and encourages the varying ministries as the leavening expands through the bread of communal life. The breath of the Spirit gives us this empowered gift. What is our identity as Christian leaders? We are the "breathed upon," the releasers.

In chapter 9, I used the analogy of the "fire-jumpers" as a metaphor for ministry. Earlier in this chapter I referred to C. S. Lewis's *The Silver Chair* in which the breath of Aslan, the great Christ lion, blows the two children into Narnia. They too are "fire-jumpers," having received their mandate to go into the hell-like underground evil kingdom. At great risk to themselves, they are to find and release the captive prince. Addicted and hypnotized by an evil spell, the prince has forgotten who he is, a royal child of the lands of light for whom a kingdom waits. The children, though full of doubt and fear, release his bonds when in his raving he calls on the name of Aslan, and they empower him to return to the lands of light.

As I watched the movie based on the book, I thought of us

Christian leaders—not better than others or superior in any way to others—who are "breathed upon" and empowered (mandated) to go into the dark prisons wherever they are and to release the bound in the name of Jesus the Christ. Jesus himself set free all those in captivity of body or spirit both before his death and after his death according to the vision in the apocryphal book Acts of Pilate. God empowers and mandates us to jump onto the burning grounds and extinguish the destructive fires of human hopelessness and woundedness, even as the living Christ surrounds us and jumps with us.

For the Christian leader, the mandate is to *do this openly in Christ's name*. This gift is not to become a secret, arcane power, hidden away within us:

> "What I say to you in the dark,
>   tell in the light" (Matt. 10:27).

Tell in the light! Suddenly for me those words take on new meaning. For me, these words call us not only to enact Christ's release openly but also to impress upon us that we are empowered and sustained only in Christ's light. We are sustained by the Breath, the living Spirit. We are sustained by the Bread, the living bread of Christ. We are sustained by the Blessing, that special energy and strength flowing from the hands of Christ—those hands whose wounds become for us the source of healing love. Thus are we shepherds fed.

REFLECTION AND MEDITATION

> "For the bread of God is that which comes down
>   from heaven
> and gives life to the world....I am the bread of life"
> (John 6:33, 35).

> "I am the gate for the sheep....I am the good shepherd....
> My sheep hear my voice. I know them, and they follow me.
> I give them eternal life....No one will snatch them out of
> my hand" (John 10:7, 11, 27-28).

Relax in whatever way is best for you, resting your body trustfully on God's strength. Take a few slow, deep breaths; then let your breathing become light and gentle.

Picture or think of the living Christ in whatever way makes the Christ most real and close to you.

Reflect for a while on Christ's invitation to become the sheep in his hand. What does it mean to you to be one of the sheep, guided and encompassed by the living Christ, the Good Shepherd? In what way do you feel fed? In what ways could you be fed more fully in daily life? What changes would this fuller nourishing suggest for you?

When ready, reflect on what it means to have been called into shepherding even while remaining Christ's sheep? How are these two conditions connected? What does this dual role mean to you personally? How can you as shepherd be fed more fully by the bread of life? What would this mean for you in practical, daily ways?

When ready, think of the disciples gathered in the locked room with the living Christ among them, breathing upon them the Holy Spirit.

Think of or picture yourself also there in that room, being breathed upon. Think of yourself now in your present room being breathed upon by the risen Christ.

Quietly breathe in that breath of empowering life. With each gentle, slow breath think of that life flowing through your whole body, enlivening every part of your body, heart, and spirit. Let the "shofar" of release sound in every bodily cell.

You may wish to pray the words of the hymn: "Breathe on me, breath of God, fill me with life anew."

When you feel ready, think of the two disciples at the inn in Emmaus. Jesus sits with them and breaks the bread and gives it to them. Picture or think of yourself with them at the table, receiving the bread. Think of yourself now in this present time and place receiving the bread from Jesus' hands.

You may wish to pray the words of the hymn:

Here would I feed upon the bread of God,
  here drink with thee the royal wine of heaven.

Sense the deep nourishment spreading through all your body, heart, and spirit.

When you feel ready, think of the disciples gathered at Bethany, looking at Jesus in what may be the last time in visible form. He lifts up his hands, the hands on which the wounds are still seen, to share with the disciples the special empowered grace from God, to share with them this strength and living Spirit. Think of yourself among them receiving that empowerment. Think of yourself now in your own time and place seeing and feeling those hands raised for *you* with the light streaming from those hands into your heart.

You may wish to pray the hymn:

Holy Spirit, truth divine, dawn upon this soul of mine....
  Holy Spirit, love divine, glow within this heart of mine.

Picture or think of the Spirit's light (which is the ongoing presence of the living Christ) glowing in your heart. Then let it become a widening circle around you, flowing from your center to all dark places.

Sense how your breathing flows slowly in and slowly out, returning to the Source, then flowing out again: just as the blood circulating through your body returns to the heart for renewal; just as the light beam receives constant renewal from the light. We cannot separate the blood from the heartbeat. We cannot separate the beam from the light. We cannot separate our own inner heart, our own inner light, from the Hand that holds them.

O Lord Jesus Christ, Thou Good Shepherd of the sheep,
  who camest to seek the lost, and to gather them into Thy
    fold,
  have compassion upon those who have wandered from Thee;
  feed those who hunger,

cause the weary to lie down in Thy pastures,
bind up those who are broken in heart,
and strengthen those who are weak,
that we, relying on Thy care
and being comforted by Thy love,
may abide in thy guidance to our lives' end—Amen.

(Ancient collect, A.D. 590)

Notes

Chapter One

1. Agnes Sanford, *Sealed Orders* (Plainfield, N.J.: Logos International, 1972), 6–7.

Chapter Two

1. Wendy M. Wright, *The Rising: Living the Mysteries of Lent, Easter, and Pentecost* (Nashville, Tenn.: Upper Room Books, 1994), 126–27.

2. G. Scott Sparrow, *I Am with You Always: True Stories of Encounters with Jesus*, Introduction by Morton Kelsey (New York: Bantam, 1995), xiv.

3. Pierre Teilhard de Chardin, *Hymn of the Universe* (New York: Harper & Row, 1961), 144.

Chapter Three

1. Ron DelBene, *The Breath of Life: A Simple Way to Pray* (Minneapolis, Minn.: Winston Press, 1981), 15–16.

2. Patricia Nolan Savas, *Gus: A Nun's Story* (South Plainfield, N.J.: Bridge Publishing Inc., 1993), 137–38.

3. Matthew Linn, Sheila Fabricant Linn, and Dennis Linn, *Healing Spiritual Abuse and Religious Addiction* (New York: Paulist Press, 1994), 11–13.

Chapter Four

1. *Hymn of the Universe*, 64–65.

2. *On the Resurrection of the Dead* as cited in *The New Christian*

Year, chosen by Charles Williams (London: Oxford University Press, 1941), 108.

3. Morton Kelsey, *The Other Side of Silence: Meditation for the Twenty-First Century* (New York: Paulist Press; 1995, 1997), 134.

4. Brennan Manning, *A Stranger to Self-Hatred: A Glimpse of Jesus* (Denville, N.J.: Dimension Books, 1982), 96–97.

5. Peter Campbell and Edwin M. McMahon, *Bio-Spirituality: Focusing As a Way to Grow* (Chicago: Loyola, 1985); 15–17, 24–25.

Chapter Five

1. William Barclay, *A Spiritual Autobiography* (Grand Rapids, Mich.: Eerdmans, 1977), 58–59.

2. Andrew Sung Park, *The Wounded Heart of God* (Nashville, Tenn.: Abingdon Press, 1993); 121, 123.

3. Leslie D. Weatherhead, *The Will of God* (Nashville, Tenn.: Abingdon Press, 1972), 11.

4. James E. Dittes, *When the People Say No: Conflict and the Call to Ministry* (SanFrancisco: Harper & Row, 1979), 59–60.

5. Conrad W. Weiser, *Healers: Harmed and Harmful* (Minneapolis, Minn.: Augsburg Fortress, 1994); 145, 152, ix.

6. James K. Wagner, *An Adventure in Healing and Wholeness* (Nashville, Tenn.: Upper Room, 1993), 91–93.

7. *The Other Side of Silence,* 255–56.

Chapter Six

1. Matthew Linn, Sheila Fabricant, Dennis Linn, *Healing the Eight Stages of Life* (Mahwah, N.J.: Paulist Press, 1988), 9.

2. *Healing the Eight Stages of Life,* 9.

Chapter Seven

1. Monica Baldwin, *I Leap over the Wall* (New York: Rinehart & Company, 1950), 219–20.

2. Evelyn Underhill, *Mysticism* (New York: The Noonday Press, 1955), 382.

3. *Mysticism,* 388.

4. *When the People Say No,* 60.

5. I highly recommend *A Farther Shore* (especially chapters 10–12) by Yvonne Rason and Teri Degler (SanFrancisco: HarperSanFrancisco, 1996) and *Transcend: A Guide to the Spiritual Quest* by Morton T. Kelsey (Paulist Press, 1981). *Transcend* is out of print but is probably available in church and public libraries.

6. "Concerning the Sacrament from Book Four," *The Imitation of Christ,* Thomas à Kempis (Hollywood, Calif.: The Marcel Rodd Company Publishers, 1945), 205–6.

Chapter Eight

1. Flora Slosson Wuellner, *Prayer, Fear, and Our Powers* (Nashville, Tenn.: Upper Room Books, 1989), 52–53.

Chapter Nine

1. *Healers: Harmed and Harmful,* 136.

2. I recommend *Clergy Killers: Guidance for Pastors and Congregations under Attack* by G. Lloyd Rediger (Westminster John Knox Press, 1997).

3. For another translation, see Anne Bancroft, *The Luminous Vision: Six Medieval Mystics and Their Teachings* (Cambridge, Mass.: Unwin Hyman, Inc., 1989), 96.

4. *Healers: Harmed and Harmful,* 141.

Chapter Ten

1. Chester P. Michael and Marie C. Norrisey, *Prayer and Temperament* (Charlottesville, Va.: The Open Door, Inc., 1984), 16.

2. Marjorie J. Thompson, *Soul Feast: An Invitation to the Christian Spiritual Life* (Louisville, Ky.: Westminster John Knox Press, 1995), 7.

Chapter Eleven

1. "Acts Of Pilate," *The Apocryphal New Testament,* trans. Montague Rhodes James (Oxford at the Clarendon Press, 1955); 134–36, 139.